BOB DYLAN THE LYRICS 1961-

THE BASEM
TAPES
地下室录音带

鲍勃·迪伦诗歌集 1961—2020
VOL.04

[美] 鲍勃·迪伦 著　李皖 译

中信出版集团 | 北京

约翰·韦斯利·哈丁
JOHN WESLEY HARDING

约翰·韦斯利·哈丁	7
一天早晨我走出门	11
我梦见我看到了圣奥古斯丁	15
沿着瞭望塔	19
弗兰基·李和犹大神父叙事曲	21
流浪汉的逃脱	29
亲爱的房东	33
我是个孤独的流浪汉	37
我同情这可怜的移民	41
奸恶的信使	45
沿着海湾走	47
沿着海湾走(另一版本)	49
今晚我会是你的宝贝	53

纳什维尔天际线
NASHVILLE SKYLINE

与你单独在一起	61
我把它全扔了	65
佩姬·白昼	67
躺下吧,姑娘,躺下	71
再过一晚	75
告诉我那不是真的	79

目录

| 乡村派 | 81 |
| 今夜我要在这儿陪你 | 85 |

---附加歌词---

| 通缉犯 | 89 |

地下室录音带
THE BASEMENT TAPES

鸡零狗碎	99
百万美元狂欢	103
去阿卡普尔科	109
看哪!	113
晾衣绳传奇	119
小苹果树	123
求你啦,亨利太太	127
愤怒的泪水	133
太多虚无	137
是啊!很重而且还有一瓶面包	141
坠入洪流	145
小蒙哥马利	149
哪儿都不去	155
不要告诉亨利	159
还什么都未交付	163
开门,荷马	167
长途接线员	171

CONTENTS

这车轮烧起来了	175

―――― 附加歌词 ――――

十字架上的名号	179
爱斯基摩人魁恩(威猛魁恩)	185
我将获得自由	189
把你的石头拿开!	193
不说话的周末	197
圣菲	201

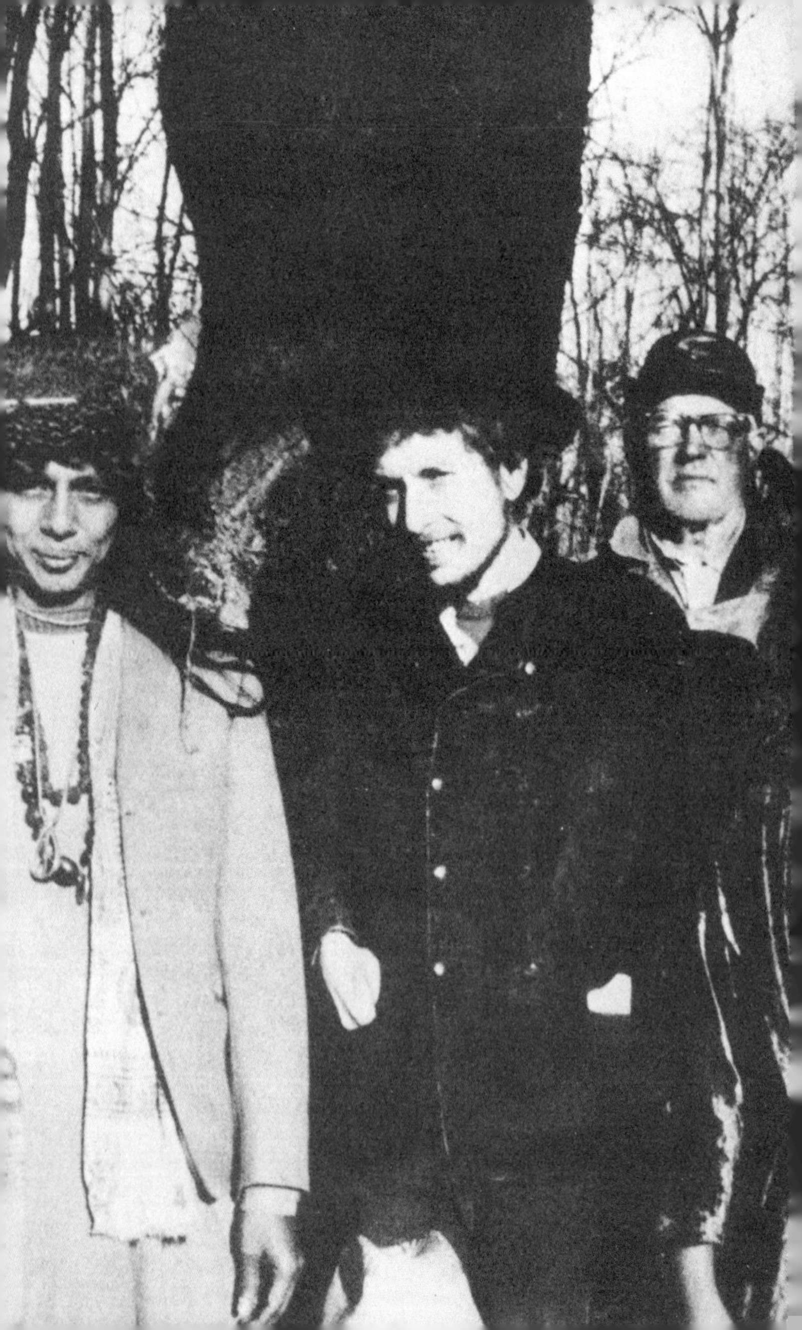

JOHN WESLEY HARDING
约翰·韦斯利·哈丁

约翰·韦斯利·哈丁

一天早晨我走出门

我梦见我看到了圣奥古斯丁

沿着瞭望塔

弗兰基·李和犹大神父叙事曲

流浪汉的逃脱

亲爱的房东

我是个孤独的流浪汉

我同情这可怜的移民

奸恶的信使

沿着海湾走

沿着海湾走（另一版本）

今晚我会是你的宝贝

i want you

the deputies they ask my name
they hide you / their ??? are
but how could i / can explain
what i want from you

your father's ghost/ he's so gaunt   he looks so
i know   they say   me he wants to haunt
  they say
& whispering what do you want   he just stares
         when he hears me
as i'm calling you
         stake

    now all my fathers theyve gone down hugging one another
    & all their daughters put me down cause i say i aint their brother

    now all my fathers/ theyve gone down/ true love, they been without it
    & all their sons & daughters put me down cause i dont think about it

drunken ~~here i stand xxxx~~ here i stand i stand here   upon the
              ~~hxxxx~~ hoping that these frozen ships   kill
    that are ~~that are dance~~ st..e madly up & down my lips   like the
                        wont fall on you   *are   (what)*

........makes his raids
        taking with him chamber m
me

      yes he's got pride
    but c'mon now   & al
                                                            t
deputies they've all the same   c
hide you, there they ask my ???
bright light   here i stand so out of
& i   with icecles
to explain
i want   dancing up & down my fa
                 that fall on you

                 cant you come/ cant you
— you
you   cant you hear me/ calli
you

1966年夏天,《金发叠金发》发行1个月后,7月29日早上,迪伦在伍德斯托克附近的小村庄发生车祸。他驾驶着凯旋500摩托车,在高速行驶中侧滑。据称,他的下侧肋骨遭到重击,颅骨受撞导致失忆,暂时性瘫痪,身体机能衰退。

10年后,迪伦回忆道:"有一天,我刚迈出半步,灯全灭了。从那时起,我或多或少失忆了……我花了很长时间,才开始能有意识地做以前无意识地做的事。"

车祸也让迪伦从密集的演唱会和唱片录制中解脱出来。他已经筋疲力尽了,精神上处于崩溃边缘。此后,他从舞台上消失了,在伍德斯托克过上了离群索居的乡村生活。恰巧"乐队"(The Band)在这里租下一个房子,进行排练和录音,这就是乐史上著名的"大粉红"(Big Pink)。在"大粉红"的地下室里,迪伦与"乐队"开始了亲密无间的默契合作。一半是玩儿,一半是为威特马克父子唱片公司提供歌曲,他和"乐队"以半专业方式录了100多首歌,史称"地下室录音带"。但创作于这一时期的专辑《约翰·韦斯利·哈丁》,并未从中摘取分毫,而是单独成稿。

迪伦的这第8张录音室专辑,由哥伦比亚唱片公司于

1967年12月27日发行。此时距《金发叠金发》的发行，已过去一年半。是自鬼门关逃生以后，迪伦第一次带来新作品。

《约翰·韦斯利·哈丁》是一张分外简肃的专辑。喧闹的乐声尽去，华丽的激情尽去，铺天盖地、意象缤纷的想象尽去，歌曲极其安静，主要只有迪伦的木吉他、口琴、钢琴和人声。

此时世界摇滚乐的舞台上，一片喧哗和轰鸣，部分也是受迪伦《金发叠金发》的影响，五色纷披、鸿篇巨制、电音此起彼伏的迷幻摇滚是时代的主旋律。而迪伦的新专辑，简短、寡言，几乎是"黑白照"。

录音在1967年10月17日、11月6日和11月29日进行，共有3场，总时长不到12个小时。

标题曲是关于距迪伦近百年之遥的得州悍匪——约翰·韦斯利·哈丁的故事。迪伦说，之所以选他做主角，是因为这个名字适合歌曲的节奏。专辑中的歌曲，像是一幅民间传说史的人物图谱：流浪汉、小丑、小偷、房东、移民、神父、信使、圣人……简单的线条、洗练的文字，除了《弗兰基·李和犹大神父叙事曲》，其他所有的歌曲都只有3段，或篇幅更短的4段，没有副歌，句子都很短。

迪伦不像过去那样放飞想象力，用放纵的方式写。他找到了新的、经济的、克制的风格，用短短3段讲述一个多幕故事。如果我们对文体更加敏感，就会发现：之前的摇滚乐，文体是布鲁斯，杂糅了现代主义诗歌；而这张专辑的文体主要是民歌。与之相应，迪伦改用成熟、干净的民歌声音演唱，第一次用颤音唱。

诗人艾伦·金斯堡（Allen Ginsberg）曾回忆：迪伦说，他希望创作一种"强力的精简歌谣"，每一行都推进叙述，"没有一个词、一口气是浪费的。每个意象都是功能性的，而不是为了装饰"。

这些歌曲远离现实，却唤起了神话般的魔力。标题曲有一种毫无疑义的真理般的敞亮，传主的行迹完全是迪伦生造的。《沿着瞭望塔》《奸恶的信使》像是直接脱胎于《圣经》，有种启示录意味，显示出天地玄黄的浩浩茫茫。《我梦见我看到了圣奥古斯丁》有沉重的负罪感，有世道翻覆的沧桑。《我同情这可怜的移民》表达了指向未来的悲凉，如《圣经》中对人类的审判和预言一般。最后两首情歌，在专辑的气氛笼罩下也都有了某种简肃和神性的意味。有专文曾列出该专辑 60 多处关于《圣经》的暗示。

但这些反向进入老美国异史的作品，每一首，又都有对现实世界和迪伦个人生活的微妙映射。比如《一天早晨我走出门》，有对他获得汤姆·潘恩奖并引发风波事件的变形镜像，深蕴着迪伦对自由运动的曲折内心活动。

在这张专辑诞生前夕，除了车祸，迪伦的个人生活里还发生了其他事件：两位朋友意外身亡；妻子生下女儿安娜；伍迪·格思里去世；迪伦与关系疏远的父母和解；与哥伦比亚唱片公司谈判，最终以一份利润丰厚的新合同结束。

JOHN WESLEY HARDING

John Wesley Harding
Was a friend to the poor
He trav'led with a gun in ev'ry hand
All along this countryside
He opened many a door
But he was never known
To hurt an honest man

'Twas down in Chaynee County
A time they talk about
With his lady by his side
He took a stand
And soon the situation there
Was all but straightened out
For he was always known
To lend a helping hand

All across the telegraph
His name it did resound

约翰·韦斯利·哈丁 [1]

约翰·韦斯利·哈丁
是穷人的朋友
他手持双枪
走遍了村野
他打开了许多门
但从没听谁说
他伤害过老实人

是在柴尼县
人们说起有一次
他带着他的女人
出来表了个态
没多久那里的局面
就都摆平了
因为大家都知道他
总是伸出援手

电报从头至尾
他的名字铮铮作响

---

[1] 约翰·韦斯利·哈丁（1853—1895），得克萨斯州著名悍匪，迪伦将其姓 Hardin 错拼为 Harding，所述也与事实不符。

But no charge held against him

Could they prove

And there was no man around

Who could track or chain him down

He was never known

To make a foolish move

但是对他的指控
一条都不能被证实
这一带没一个人
能尾随和拿获他
从没听谁说
他踏错一步

AS I WENT OUT ONE MORNING

As I went out one morning
To breathe the air around Tom Paine's
I spied the fairest damsel
That ever did walk in chains
I offer'd her my hand
She took me by the arm
I knew that very instant
She meant to do me harm

"Depart from me this moment"
I told her with my voice
Said she, "But I don't wish to"
Said I, "But you have no choice"
"I beg you, sir," she pleaded
From the corners of her mouth
"I will secretly accept you
And together we'll fly south"

一天早晨我走出门

一天早晨我走出门
呼吸汤姆·潘恩[1]家周围的空气
发现了那个曾戴枷行走的
最为美丽的女子
我向她伸出手去
她挽住了我的胳膊
一瞬间我明白过来
她想加害我

"马上离开我"
我用声音告诉她
她说:"可是我不想"
我说:"可你别无选择"
"我求你了,先生"
她从嘴角边,恳求道
"我会偷偷接受你
我们一起飞往南方"

---

[1] 1963年,迪伦被授予汤姆·潘恩公民权利奖。汤姆·潘恩(1737—1809)是英裔美国思想家、作家、政治活动家,参加了美国独立运动和法国大革命。在颁奖仪式上,迪伦发表了即兴演讲,切割了自己与知识界的关系。

Just then Tom Paine, himself
Came running from across the field
Shouting at this lovely girl
And commanding her to yield
And as she was letting go her grip
Up Tom Paine did run
"I'm sorry, sir," he said to me
"I'm sorry for what she's done"

就在这时,汤姆·潘恩本人
从田野另一边跑来
冲这个可爱的姑娘大喊
命她退下
当她放开手
汤姆·潘恩跑到了面前
"对不起,先生,"他对我说
"我为她的行为感到抱歉"

I DREAMED I SAW ST. AUGUSTINE

I dreamed I saw St. Augustine

Alive as you or me

Tearing through these quarters

In the utmost misery

With a blanket underneath his arm

And a coat of solid gold

Searching for the very souls

Whom already have been sold

"Arise, arise," he cried so loud

In a voice without restraint

"Come out, ye gifted kings and queens

And hear my sad complaint

No martyr is among ye now

Whom you can call your own

So go on your way accordingly

But know you're not alone"

I dreamed I saw St. Augustine

我梦见我看到了圣奥古斯丁[1]

我梦见我看到了圣奥古斯丁
跟你我一样活着
他匆匆穿过一间间院舍
模样极度痛苦
他穿着纯金外套
腋下夹一条毯子
他在搜寻那些
已经被卖掉的灵魂

"起来,起来,"他大声喊着
声音里全无克制
"出来吧,真命的君王和王后们
来听听我的悲诉
现在你们中间已没有殉道者了
属于你们的殉道者
所以继续这么走下去吧
但是要知道,你们并不孤独"

我梦见我看到了圣奥古斯丁

---

[1] 圣奥古斯丁(354—430),神学家和哲学家,著有《忏悔录》,帮助建立了原罪学说。本篇由杨盈盈校译。

Alive with fiery breath
And I dreamed I was amongst the ones
That put him out to death
Oh, I awoke in anger
So alone and terrified
I put my fingers against the glass
And bowed my head and cried

活着，呼吸如火
我梦见我就在众人之中
一起把他逼上了死路
啊，我愤怒地醒来了
如此孤独和恐惧
用手指挡着镜子
埋下了头哭泣

ALL ALONG THE WATCHTOWER

"There must be some way out of here," said the joker to the thief
"There's too much confusion, I can't get no relief
Businessmen, they drink my wine, plowmen dig my earth
None of them along the line know what any of it is worth"

"No reason to get excited," the thief, he kindly spoke
"There are many here among us who feel that life is but a joke
But you and I, we've been through that, and this is not our fate
So let us not talk falsely now, the hour is getting late"

All along the watchtower, princes kept the view
While all the women came and went, barefoot servants, too

Outside in the distance a wildcat did growl
Two riders were approaching, the wind began to howl

沿着瞭望塔

"此地一定有出路,"小丑对
 小偷说
"可实在太混乱,我无法歇口气
商人们喝我的酒,农夫们挖我的地
他们当中没人知道这些东西的价值"

"没必要这么激动,"小偷和善地说
"好多人觉得生活就是个玩笑
但是你我已过了那个阶段,这不该是咱俩的命
所以别说没用的了,时辰已经不早了"

沿着瞭望塔,王子们一直张望
女人们和赤脚的仆人,来来往往

远处一只野猫在咆哮
两个骑手渐渐走近,风开始呼啸

THE BALLAD OF FRANKIE LEE AND JUDAS PRIEST

Well, Frankie Lee and Judas Priest
They were the best of friends
So when Frankie Lee needed money one day
Judas quickly pulled out a roll of tens
And placed them on a footstool
Just above the plotted plain
Sayin', "Take your pick, Frankie Boy
My loss will be your gain"

Well, Frankie Lee, he sat right down
And put his fingers to his chin
But with the cold eyes of Judas on him
His head began to spin
"Would ya please not stare at me like that," he said
"It's just my foolish pride
But sometimes a man must be alone
And this is no place to hide"

Well, Judas, he just winked and said
"All right, I'll leave you here
But you'd better hurry up and choose which of those bills you want

弗兰基·李和犹大神父叙事曲

哦,弗兰基·李和犹大神父
他们是最要好的朋友
所以有天弗兰基·李需要钱
犹大当即掏出一卷十元钞票
搁在脚凳上
就在那片划成一块块儿的平原间
说:"随便拿,弗兰基兄弟
我的损失就是你的收益"

哦,弗兰基·李,端坐下来
把手指放在下巴处
但在犹大冷冷的目光下
他的头开始发晕
"能不能不这么盯着我,"他说
"这只是我愚蠢的自尊吧
但有时候人必须独处
这里无处可躲"

哦,犹大,他眨眨眼说
"好吧,我不打扰你
但你最好快点,选好你想要的
　钞票

Before they all disappear"
"I'm gonna start my pickin' right now
Just tell me where you'll be"
Judas pointed down the road
And said, "Eternity!"

"Eternity?" said Frankie Lee
With a voice as cold as ice
"That's right," said Judas Priest, "Eternity
Though you might call it 'Paradise'"
"I don't call it anything"
Said Frankie Lee with a smile
"All right," said Judas Priest
"I'll see you after a while"

Well, Frankie Lee, he sat back down
Feelin' low and mean
When just then a passing stranger
Burst upon the scene
Saying, "Are you Frankie Lee, the gambler
Whose father is deceased?
Well, if you are, there's a fellow callin' you down the road
And they say his name is Priest"

"Oh, yes, he is my friend"
Said Frankie Lee in fright

免得它们跑掉"
"我现在就开始拿
不过告诉我你去哪儿"
犹大指了指路
说:"去永恒!"

"永恒?"弗兰基·李说
声音冷得像冰
"对,"犹大神父说,"永恒
虽然你可能叫它'天堂'"
"我什么都不叫"
弗兰基·李笑着说
"好吧,"犹大神父说
"咱过会儿见"

哦,弗兰基·李,又坐回去
情绪低落,有点闷闷不乐
就在这时一个路过的陌生人
突然出现在面前
说:"你就是弗兰基·李
那个父亲过世了的赌徒?
哦,如果你是,有个伙计在路上叫你
他们说他名叫神父"

"噢,是的,他是我朋友"
弗兰基·李吃一惊

"I do recall him very well
In fact, he just left my sight"
"Yes, that's the one," said the stranger
As quiet as a mouse
"Well, my message is, he's down the road
Stranded in a house"

Well, Frankie Lee, he panicked
He dropped ev'rything and ran
Until he came up to the spot
Where Judas Priest did stand
"What kind of house is this," he said
"Where I have come to roam?"
"It's not a house," said Judas Priest
"It's not a house . . . it's a home"

Well, Frankie Lee, he trembled
He soon lost all control
Over ev'rything which he had made
While the mission bells did toll
He just stood there staring
At that big house as bright as any sun
With four and twenty windows
And a woman's face in ev'ry one

Well, up the stairs ran Frankie Lee

"我当然记得他
事实上,他刚才还在我这里"
"是的,就是那个人,"陌生人说
像老鼠一样平静
"哦,我的口信是,他就在这路上
被困在一幢房子里"

哦,弗兰基·李慌了
他丢下东西就跑
一直跑到那地方
犹大神父站在那儿
"这是什么房子,"他问
"我这是在哪儿游荡?"
"这不是房子,"犹大神父说
"这不是房子……这是家"

哦,弗兰基·李颤抖了
他一下就失去了控制
忘了自己在做什么
当教堂的钟响起时
他只是站那儿瞪着
那幢像太阳一样明亮的大房子
有二十四扇窗
每扇窗里都有一张女人的脸

哦,弗兰基·李跑上楼去

With a soulful, bounding leap
And, foaming at the mouth
He began to make his midnight creep
For sixteen nights and days he raved
But on the seventeenth he burst
Into the arms of Judas Priest
Which is where he died of thirst

No one tried to say a thing
When they took him out in jest
Except, of course, the little neighbor boy
Who carried him to rest
And he just walked along, alone
With his guilt so well concealed
And muttered underneath his breath
"Nothing is revealed"

Well, the moral of the story
The moral of this song
Is simply that one should never be
Where one does not belong
So when you see your neighbor carryin' somethin'
Help him with his load
And don't go mistaking Paradise
For that home across the road

以一种灵魂般的向上的跳跃
然后，口中流沫
他开始在半夜幽幽走动 [1]
十六个昼夜都在胡言乱语
但是在第十七天，他猛然投入
犹大神父的怀抱
就在那里干渴而死

没有一个人想说话
当人们说笑着带走他
当然，除了那个背着他去安息的
邻居家的小男孩
他就这么走着，一个人
把他的罪好好藏着
比呼吸还低地嘟哝
"什么都没泄露"

哦，这个故事的寓意
这首歌的寓意，非常简单
一个人永远不该
去不属于他的地方
因此当你看到邻居在搬东西
请帮他一把
再就是别把天堂
误以为是马路对面的家

---

[1] 半夜幽幽走动，又有"寻欢"之意。

DRIFTER'S ESCAPE

"Oh, help me in my weakness"
I heard the drifter say
As they carried him from the courtroom
And were taking him away
"My trip hasn't been a pleasant one
And my time it isn't long
And I still do not know
What it was that I've done wrong"

Well, the judge, he cast his robe aside
A tear came to his eye
"You fail to understand," he said
"Why must you even try?"
Outside, the crowd was stirring
You could hear it from the door
Inside, the judge was stepping down
While the jury cried for more

"Oh, stop that cursed jury"
Cried the attendant and the nurse
"The trial was bad enough
But this is ten times worse"

流浪汉的逃脱

"啊,帮帮我,除掉我的缺点"
我听到那流浪汉说
当他们将他架出庭
要带走他
"我的旅程不愉快
而且我时间不多了
我仍没搞清楚
我做错了什么"

嗯,法官,把法袍扔一边
一颗泪珠涌上老眼
"你理解不了,"他说
"你何必要理解?"
外面,人群骚动
隔着门都能听见
里面,法官走下来
而陪审团嚷嚷着要重判

"啊,该死的陪审团,拉倒吧"
侍者和护士喊
"判决已经够糟了
陪审团还要更糟十倍"

Just then a bolt of lightning
Struck the courthouse out of shape
And while ev'rybody knelt to pray
The drifter did escape

恰在此时一道闪电

击垮了法院大楼

每个人都跪下祷告

流浪汉就在此时，逃之夭夭

DEAR LANDLORD

Dear landlord
Please don't put a price on my soul
My burden is heavy
My dreams are beyond control
When that steamboat whistle blows
I'm gonna give you all I got to give
And I do hope you receive it well
Dependin' on the way you feel that you live

Dear landlord
Please heed these words that I speak
I know you've suffered much
But in this you are not so unique
All of us, at times, we might work too hard
To have it too fast and too much
And anyone can fill his life up
With things he can see but he just cannot touch

Dear landlord
Please don't dismiss my case
I'm not about to argue
I'm not about to move to no other place

亲爱的房东

亲爱的房东
请不要给我的灵魂定价
我的担子很重
我的梦不听管束
当那汽船拉响汽笛时
我就会付清我该给的
真希望你妥妥地收到
这取决于你如何看待你的生活

亲爱的房东
请注意我说的
我知道你已经受够了
但在这点上你并不特别
有时候我们每个人,都有可能太过于努力
以至不能太快太好地达成目的
而每个人都能够
以他看得见却摸不着的东西,填满生活

亲爱的房东
请不要驳斥我
我不想吵架
我也不打算搬家

Now, each of us has his own special gift
And you know this was meant to be true
And if you don't underestimate me
I won't underestimate you

你看，我们都有自己的特殊禀赋
你知道这肯定是真的
如果你不小看我
我也不会小看你

I AM A LONESOME HOBO

I am a lonesome hobo
Without family or friends
Where another man's life might begin
That's exactly where mine ends
I have tried my hand at bribery
Blackmail and deceit
And I've served time for ev'rything
'Cept beggin' on the street

Well, once I was rather prosperous
There was nothing I did lack
I had fourteen-karat gold in my mouth
And silk upon my back
But I did not trust my brother
I carried him to blame
Which led me to my fatal doom
To wander off in shame

Kind ladies and kind gentlemen
Soon I will be gone
But let me just warn you all
Before I do pass on

我是个孤独的流浪汉

我是个孤独的流浪汉
没有家人和友伴
别人生活开始之处
却是我生活的终点
我亲手行过贿
干过勒索搞过诈骗
因种种勾当坐牢
唯独没因为街头行乞犯过案

嗯,我也有过好时光
应有尽有啥都不缺
嘴里镶了 14K 的金牙
身上穿着绸缎绫罗
可我不信任我兄弟
我害他背了黑锅
要命的厄运由此开始
将我引向耻辱的流浪之途

好心的女士好心的先生
很快我就会离去
但在我告别之前
允许我奉劝诸位

Stay free from petty jealousies
Live by no man's code
And hold your judgment for yourself
Lest you wind up on this road

请远离嫉妒
勿以他人原则生活
坚持自己的判断
否则你就会走上这条路

I PITY THE POOR IMMIGRANT

I pity the poor immigrant
Who wishes he would've stayed home
Who uses all his power to do evil
But in the end is always left so alone
That man whom with his fingers cheats
And who lies with ev'ry breath
Who passionately hates his life
And likewise, fears his death

I pity the poor immigrant
Whose strength is spent in vain
Whose heaven is like Ironsides
Whose tears are like rain
Who eats but is not satisfied
Who hears but does not see
Who falls in love with wealth itself
And turns his back on me

I pity the poor immigrant
Who tramples through the mud
Who fills his mouth with laughing
And who builds his town with blood

我同情这可怜的移民

我同情这可怜的移民
他幻想着仍留在故乡
使足了力量作恶
到头来却还是孤独一人
这人用巧手去坑骗
呼吸之间全是谎言
强烈憎恶着自己的生活
同样地,惧怕着自己的死亡

我同情这可怜的移民
他的力气用于虚无
他的天堂像铁甲舰队
他的泪水恍若雨水
他吃但不知足
他听但不懂得
他爱,爱上的是财富
却转过背来对着我

我同情这可怜的移民
他踏过一路的泥
他嘴里塞满了笑
他用血造他的城

Whose visions in the final end

Must shatter like the glass

I pity the poor immigrant

When his gladness comes to pass

这幻影在最后
必将如玻璃般粉碎
我同情这可怜的移民
当他的欢喜得以成真

THE WICKED MESSENGER

There was a wicked messenger
From Eli he did come
With a mind that multiplied the smallest matter
When questioned who had sent for him
He answered with his thumb
For his tongue it could not speak, but only flatter

He stayed behind the assembly hall
It was there he made his bed
Oftentimes he could be seen returning
Until one day he just appeared
With a note in his hand which read
"The soles of my feet, I swear they're burning"

Oh, the leaves began to fallin'
And the seas began to part
And the people that confronted him were many
And he was told but these few words
Which opened up his heart
"If ye cannot bring good news, then don't bring any"

奸恶的信使

有一个奸恶的信使
确从以利那处来
有颗将最小的事放大的心
当被问及谁指派他
他用大拇指作答
因为他的舌头不会说话,只会奉承

他待在会议厅后面
就在那儿搭了床
时常可以见他回来
直到有一天,他出现了
手里有张纸,写着
"我的脚底,我发誓它在燃烧"

啊,树叶开始落
大海开始分开
许多人和他面对着
他只被告知一句话
洞穿了他的心扉
"如果不能带来好消息,就什么都别带了"

DOWN ALONG THE COVE

Down along the cove
I spied my true love comin' my way
Down along the cove
I spied my true love comin' my way
I say, "Lord, have mercy, mama
It sure is good to see you comin' today"

Down along the cove
I spied my little bundle of joy
Down along the cove
I spied my little bundle of joy
She said, "Lord, have mercy, honey
I'm so glad you're my boy!"

Down along the cove
We walked together hand in hand
Down along the cove
We walked together hand in hand
Ev'rybody watchin' us go by
Knows we're in love, yes, and they understand

沿着海湾走

沿着海湾走
我看见真爱向我走来
沿着海湾走
我看见真爱向我走来
我说:"天可怜见,妈妈
看到你今天来真是太好了"

沿着海湾走
我看见我的小亲亲
沿着海湾走
我看见我的小亲亲
她说:"天可怜见,小宝贝儿
你做我的男友我好开心!"

沿着海湾走
我们俩手牵着手
沿着海湾走
我们俩手牵着手
每个人看着我们走过
知道我们在相爱,是的,他们都懂

DOWN ALONG THE COVE
(ALTERNATE VERSION)

Down along the cove I spied my little bundle of joy
Down along the cove I spied my little bundle of joy
I said, "Lord have mercy, baby
You make me feel just like a baby boy"

Down along the cove a bunch of people are milling around
Down along the cove a bunch of people are milling around
I said, "Lord have mercy, baby, they're gonna knock you when you're up
They're gonna kick you when you're down"

Down along the cove I feel as high as a bird
Down along the cove I feel as high as a bird
I said, "Lord have mercy, baby
How come you never say more than a word?"

Down along the cove I seen the Jacks and the River Queen
Down along the cove I seen the Jacks and the River Queen
I said, "Lord have mercy, baby
Ain't that the biggest boat you ever seen?"

沿着海湾走
(另一版本)

沿着海湾走我看见我的小可爱
沿着海湾走我看见我的小可爱
我说:"天可怜见,宝贝
你让我觉得自己就像个小男孩"

沿着海湾走一帮人在转来转去
沿着海湾走一帮人在转来转去
我说:"天可怜见,宝贝,你起来时他们
　　踩你
下去时他们踢你"

沿着海湾走我觉得像鸟高飞
沿着海湾走我觉得像鸟高飞
我说:"天可怜见,宝贝
怎么你每次都只说一个字?"

沿着海湾走我看到水兵与"河女王"号
沿着海湾走我看到水兵与"河女王"号
我说:"天可怜见,宝贝
那难道不是你见过的最大的船?"

Down along the cove, you can lay all your money down
Down along the cove, you can lay all your money down
I said, "Lord have mercy, baby
Ain't it a shame how they shove you and they push you around?"

Down along the cove, I got my suitcase in my hand
Down along the cove, I got my suitcase in my hand
I said, "Lord have mercy, baby
Ain't you glad that I'm your man?"

沿着海湾走,你可以把所有钱放下
沿着海湾走,你可以把所有钱放下
我说:"天可怜见,宝贝
他们把你推来推去这岂不是很
   丢脸?"

沿着海湾走,我手上拎着行李
沿着海湾走,我手上拎着行李
我说:"天可怜见,宝贝
我是你的男人,你难道不开心?"

I'LL BE YOUR BABY TONIGHT

Close your eyes, close the door
You don't have to worry anymore
I'll be your baby tonight

Shut the light, shut the shade
You don't have to be afraid
I'll be your baby tonight

Well, that mockingbird's gonna sail away
We're gonna forget it
That big, fat moon is gonna shine like a spoon
But we're gonna let it
You won't regret it

Kick your shoes off, do not fear
Bring that bottle over here
I'll be your baby tonight

今晚我会是你的宝贝

闭上眼,关上门
不用再担心
今晚我会是你的宝贝

关上灯,放下窗帘
不必再害怕
今晚我会是你的宝贝

好,那只嘲笑鸟要飞走了
我们会将它忘记
那又大又肥的月亮会像勺子一样发光
不过我们会由它去
你不会后悔

踢掉鞋,不怕
把那瓶酒拿到这里
今晚我会是你的宝贝

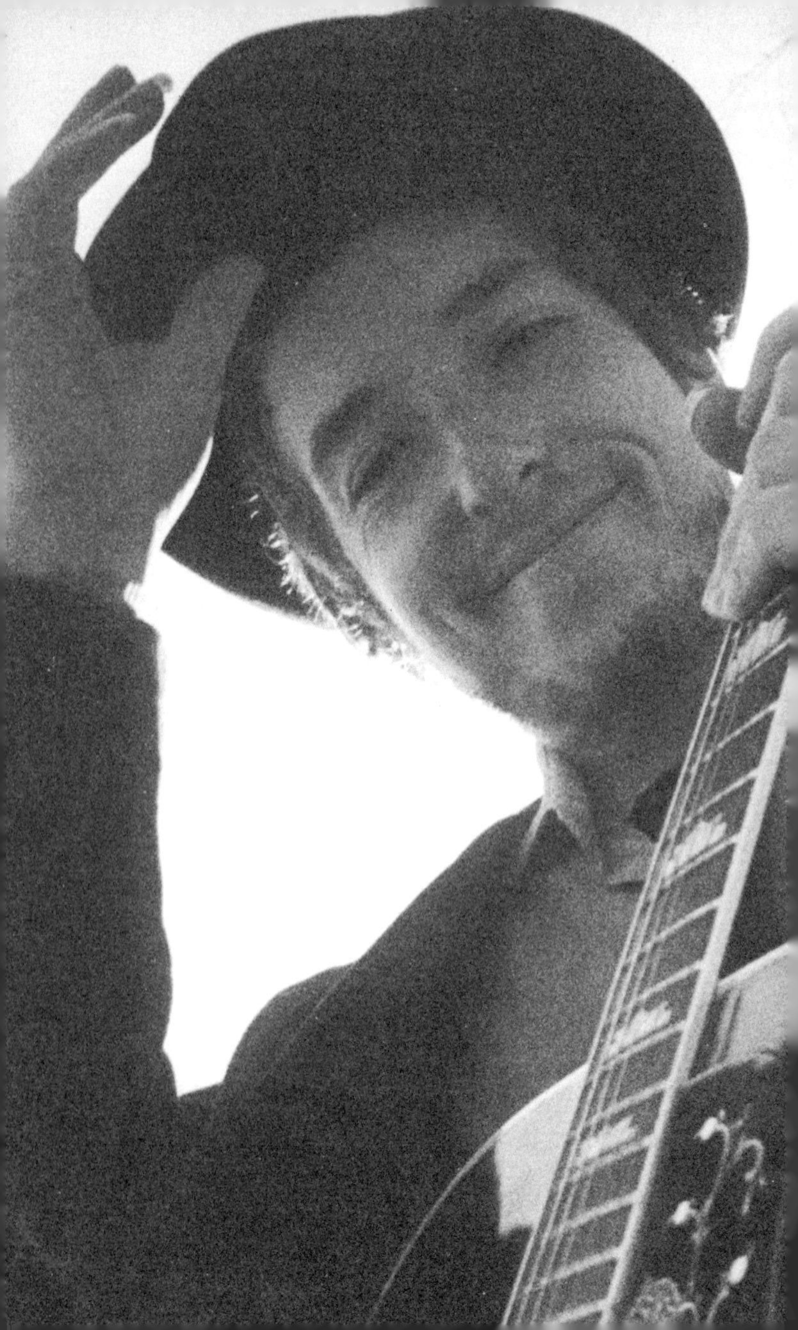

NASHVILLE SKYLINE
纳什维尔天际线

与你单独在一起

我把它全扔了

佩姬·白昼

躺下吧,姑娘,躺下

再过一晚

告诉我那不是真的

乡村派

今夜我要在这儿陪你

附加歌词 ——————————

通缉犯

1. Throw my ticket out the window
   Throw my suitcase out there too
   Throw my troubles out the door -
   I don't need them anymore
   Cause tonight I'm staying here with you

《纳什维尔天际线》,迪伦的第 9 张录音室专辑,于 1969 年 4 月 9 日由哥伦比亚唱片公司发行。

距离上一张专辑《约翰·韦斯利·哈丁》,时间又过去了 15 个月。迪伦一直待在伍德斯托克的家,除了 1968 年 1 月 20 日去卡内基音乐厅参加了两场纪念格思里的音乐会,他很少出门。与妻子和 3 个孩子的恬静生活,唯一一次被打破,是三子——生于 1968 年 7 月的塞缪尔——因心脏病夭亡。

家庭生活之外,迪伦照常与"乐队"在"大粉红"进行即兴演奏。一些新歌逐渐形成。

此时,美国政治更加两极分化。1968 年,民权运动领袖马丁·路德·金、总统候选人罗伯特·F. 肯尼迪先后遭暗杀。大多数主要城市爆发骚乱。1969 年 1 月,新总统尼克松就职,越南战争持续、学生抗议、公民权运动及各种抗议活动此起彼伏。迪伦是青年运动的标志人物,即使他远离了流行中心,他也从未失去自己的文化地位。相形之下,乡村音乐是保守主义的象征,纳什维尔简直代表反动,如迪伦传记作者克林顿·海林(Clinton Heylin)所言:"如果迪伦担心摇滚选民的支持,那么在纳什维尔与约翰尼·卡什一起制作专辑，在许多人看来就等于退位。"

《纳什维尔天际线》在"乡村音乐之都"录制。1969年2月13、14、17和18日，迪伦邀来曾几度合作的纳什维尔音乐好手，并将队伍扩展，一起进行了4场录音。这回迪伦深思熟虑，带来的都是歌曲成品。多年后，他在接受采访时说："我们就是录一首歌，我负责唱，其他人把各自最拿手的东西表现出来就行了。同时，录音师在控制室进行调控，尽可能捕捉到最好的素材。这就是我们要做的，仅此而已。"

专辑制作完成，9首歌加1首器乐曲，竟只有26分46秒。这就是专辑的总长！主打曲目——与约翰尼·卡什二重唱的《北国姑娘》——是6年前的旧曲。

《纳什维尔天际线》展现了迪伦对乡村音乐的沉浸。主题简单，歌曲简单，更令人意外的是歌声，完全不像是迪伦的声音。他在用一种柔和的、不乏做作的乡村嗓音演唱。迪伦戒烟了。"不再吸烟以后，我的嗓音就变了，事情就是这么简单。我自己也不敢相信，但这是真的。"迪伦说。

最终，令听众感到意外的，是专辑整体的氛围——非常安详，绝对乐观，近乎无欲无求。《公告牌》的埃德·奥克斯（Ed Ochs）讥讽道："心满意足的男人说着陈词滥调，脸红得就像每天都是情人节一样。"英国评论家蒂姆·苏斯特（Tim Souster）话里有话："人们情不自禁地感觉少了点什么。这田园诗般的乡村风景是不是太美了，不像是真的？"

两极化评论的另一极，比如，音乐评论家罗伯特·克里斯戈（Robert Christgau）指出：迪伦再次玩弄了公众的期望，采用了乡村男高音的声音和审美；这张专辑的美妙在于歌曲"完全不高的要求"和"单一的品质"。

《纳什维尔天际线》是迪伦的巨大转向。即使与上一张似乎同样轻描淡写的《约翰·韦斯利·哈丁》相比，它也完全不一样。这里不再有暗讽，不再有寓意，不再有教育意义，就是一些爱的歌曲。这些爱也没有思考，就是爱的生活和情感本身，这才是即使到今天，也仍然让我们感到意外之处。这些歌词似有一种真正的纯粹，毫无一丝杂念，甚至也不需要任何技巧来装点，爱的生活和情感凭自身成立。它让我联想到，艺术并不非得需要奇异，生活本身是值得的，快乐不需要深刻也一样可以成为艺术的主旨，也极为有趣并且有人性，十分精彩。

《纳什维尔天际线》完全就是乡村音乐。它是如此恬静，时代的喧嚣、社会的动荡仿佛被过滤了。与前作相比，这或许是迪伦出道以来最轻、最微不足道的专辑，却对文化流向产生了重大影响。迪伦的独立自我和独立思考，像是以轻言细语，震撼了人声鼎沸的 20 世纪 60 年代末。创作歌手克里斯·克里斯托弗森（Kris Kristofferson）说："他（迪伦）改变了人们的思考方式——甚至老式大剧院也不再一样了。"动荡年代像是在此转了弯，此后越来越多的艺人跟随迪伦的脚步，走向了寂静的乡野和质朴的生活。20 世纪 70 年代来了。

TO BE ALONE WITH YOU

To be alone with you
Just you and me
Now won't you tell me true
Ain't that the way it oughta be?
To hold each other tight
The whole night through
Ev'rything is always right
When I'm alone with you

To be alone with you
At the close of the day
With only you in view
While evening slips away
It only goes to show
That while life's pleasures be few
The only one I know
Is when I'm alone with you

They say that nighttime is the right time
To be with the one you love
Too many thoughts get in the way in the day
But you're always what I'm thinkin' of

与你单独在一起

与你单独在一起
就只有我和你
就不能给句真话吗
难道不该如此?
紧紧地拥抱在一起
长夜就这样过去
一切都是对的
当与你单独在一起

与你单独在一起
白天行将结束
我的视线中只有你
黄昏在悄然逝去
这一切不过是表明
人生乐趣无多
而我知道的唯一乐事
是与你单独在一起

人说夜晚才是佳时
与所爱的人共度
白天总是千头万绪
虽然你始终在我心底

I wish the night were here
Bringin' me all of your charms
When only you are near
To hold me in your arms

I'll always thank the Lord
When my working day's through
I get my sweet reward
To be alone with you

多希望眼前就是晚上
它带来你的千般姿容
只你在身旁
将我拥入怀中

我会时时称颂主上
当劳作的一日过去
我就会得到那甜美的奖赏
与你单独在一起

I THREW IT ALL AWAY

I once held her in my arms
She said she would always stay
But I was cruel
I treated her like a fool
I threw it all away

Once I had mountains in the palm of my hand
And rivers that ran through ev'ry day
I must have been mad
I never knew what I had
Until I threw it all away

Love is all there is, it makes the world go 'round
Love and only love, it can't be denied
No matter what you think about it
You just won't be able to do without it
Take a tip from one who's tried

So if you find someone that gives you all of her love
Take it to your heart, don't let it stray
For one thing that's certain
You will surely be a-hurtin'
If you throw it all away

我把它全扔了

我曾经拥她入怀
她说她将永远留在这儿
但是我太残忍
当她是傻瓜
我把它全扔了

以前我掌心有山岳
还有江河日夜奔腾
我一定是疯了
不明白我拥有的
直到我把它全扔了

爱就是一切,使世界运转
爱且仅有爱,无法被否定
不管你看法如何
没有它你将寸步难行
来,听这过来人的叮咛

所以如果你找到全心爱你的人
把她搁心里,不要弄丢了
因为有一桩事极为确定
你一定会伤很深
假如你把它都扔了

PEGGY DAY

Peggy Day stole my poor heart away
By golly, what more can I say
Love to spend the night with Peggy Day

Peggy night makes my future look so bright
Man, that girl is out of sight
Love to spend the day with Peggy night

Well, you know that even before I learned her name
You know I loved her just the same
An' I tell 'em all, wherever I may go
Just so they'll know, that she's my little lady
And I love her so

Peggy Day stole my poor heart away
Turned my skies to blue from gray
Love to spend the night with Peggy Day

Peggy Day stole my poor heart away

佩姬·白昼 [1]

佩姬·白昼偷走了我可怜的心
天哪,我还能说什么
多想和佩姬·白昼一起过夜

夜晚的佩姬让我的未来一片光明
嘿,这姑娘根本看不见
多想和夜晚的佩姬共度白天

好吧,你知道甚至在我知晓她名字以前
你知道我就这样爱她
我告诉每一个人,无论我走到哪儿
他们都要知道,她是我的小女人
我是如此爱她

佩姬·白昼偷走了我可怜的心
把我的天从灰色变成蓝色
多想和佩姬·白昼一起过夜

佩姬·白昼偷走了我可怜的心

---

[1] 女子名佩姬·黛(Peggy Day),字面上有佩姬·白天的意思,迪伦由此生发联想,有了这首歌词。

By golly, what more can I say
Love to spend the night with Peggy Day
Love to spend the night with Peggy Day

天哪，我还能说什么
多想和佩姬·白昼一起过夜
多想和佩姬·白昼一起过夜

LAY, LADY, LAY

Lay, lady, lay, lay across my big brass bed
Lay, lady, lay, lay across my big brass bed
Whatever colors you have in your mind
I'll show them to you and you'll see them shine

Lay, lady, lay, lay across my big brass bed
Stay, lady, stay, stay with your man awhile
Until the break of day, let me see you make him smile
His clothes are dirty but his hands are clean
And you're the best thing that he's ever seen

Stay, lady, stay, stay with your man awhile
Why wait any longer for the world to begin
You can have your cake and eat it too
Why wait any longer for the one you love
When he's standing in front of you

Lay, lady, lay, lay across my big brass bed
Stay, lady, stay, stay while the night is still ahead

躺下吧，姑娘，躺下

躺下吧，姑娘，躺下，躺在我大大的铜床上
躺下吧，姑娘，躺下，躺在我大大的铜床上
不管你心里有什么颜色
我都会让你看到，看到它们闪闪发光

躺下吧，姑娘，躺下，躺在我大大的铜床上
留下吧，姑娘，留下，与你的男人待一会儿
一直到天破晓，让我看见你让他微笑
他的衣服很脏，但他的手干干净净
而你是他见过的最美的风景

留下吧，姑娘，留下，与你的男人待一会儿
何必等太久，等这世界开始
你有蛋糕，当然也可以将它吃掉 [1]
何必等太久，等你所爱的人
此时此刻他正站在面前

躺下吧，姑娘，躺下，躺在我大大的铜床上
留下吧，姑娘，留下，当长夜漫漫还在远方

---

[1] "你有蛋糕，当然你也可以将它吃掉"，化用英语中的成语，意思是"鱼和熊掌并非不可兼得"。

I long to see you in the morning light
I long to reach for you in the night
Stay, lady, stay, stay while the night is still ahead

我渴望在晨光中见到你
我渴望在黑夜里够到你
留下吧,姑娘,留下,当长夜漫漫还在远方

ONE MORE NIGHT

One more night, the stars are in sight
But tonight I'm as lonesome as can be
Oh, the moon is shinin' bright
Lighting ev'rything in sight
But tonight no light will shine on me

Oh, it's shameful and it's sad I lost the only pal I had
I just could not be what she wanted me to be
I will turn my head up high
To that dark and rolling sky
For tonight no light will shine on me

I was so mistaken when I thought that she'd be true
I had no idea what a woman in love would do!

One more night, I will wait for the light
While the wind blows high above the tree
Oh, I miss my darling so
I didn't mean to see her go
But tonight no light will shine on me

One more night, the moon is shinin' bright

再过一晚

只要再过一晚,就会看见星光
但是在今晚,我的心无比荒凉
啊,月亮明澈地照射
点亮视野中的一切
但是今晚的光,不会照到我身上

啊,多么屈辱和悲伤,失去了唯一的同伴
我就是做不到她希望我的那样
我于是把头高昂着
迎向那黑暗翻滚的天
因为今晚的光,不会照到我身上

我错得多离谱啊,以为她真真实实
完全不知道恋爱中的女人会做出什么!

只要再过一晚,我等着那光亮
那时会有风在树上高高飞扬
啊,多思念我的爱
我不是有意要看她离开
但是今晚的光,不会照到我身上

只要再过一晚,月亮将明澈地照射

And the wind blows high above the tree

Oh, I miss that woman so

I didn't mean to see her go

But tonight no light will shine on me

而风也会在树上高高飞扬
啊,多思念我的爱
我不是有意要看她离开
但是今晚的光,不会照到我身上

TELL ME THAT IT ISN'T TRUE

I have heard rumors all over town
They say that you're planning to put me down
All I would like you to do
Is tell me that it isn't true

They say that you've been seen with some other man
That he's tall, dark and handsome, and you're holding his hand
Darlin', I'm a-countin' on you
Tell me that it isn't true

To know that some other man is holdin' you tight
It hurts me all over, it doesn't seem right

All of those awful things that I have heard
I don't want to believe them, all I want is your word
So darlin', you better come through
Tell me that it isn't true

All of those awful things that I have heard
I don't want to believe them, all I want is your word
So darlin', I'm countin' on you
Tell me that it isn't true

告诉我那不是真的

我听到谣言满城飞
说你正打算甩了我
我只希望你做件事
告诉我那不是真的

传言说看见你跟别的男人在一起
他魁梧黝黑英俊,而你的手牵着他的
亲爱的,我就靠你了
告诉我那不是真的

得知别的男人紧紧地拉着你
我浑身都疼,这样好像不行

传言中那些可怕的事
我都不愿信,我只要听你说
所以亲爱的,你最好说实话
告诉我那不是真的

传言中那些可怕的事
我都不愿信,我只要听你说
所以亲爱的,我就靠你了
告诉我那不是真的

COUNTRY PIE

Just like old Saxophone Joe
When he's got the hogshead up on his toe
Oh me, oh my
Love that country pie

Listen to the fiddler play
When he's playin' 'til the break of day
Oh me, oh my
Love that country pie

Raspberry, strawberry, lemon and lime
What do I care?
Blueberry, apple, cherry, pumpkin and plum
Call me for dinner, honey, I'll be there

Saddle me up my big white goose
Tie me on 'er and turn her loose
Oh me, oh my
Love that country pie

I don't need much and that ain't no lie
Ain't runnin' any race

乡村派

就像萨克斯手老乔
当他一口灌下了一桶酒
天,天哪
我爱死了那个乡村派

听提琴手狂奏
一奏就到了天明
天,天哪
我爱死了那个乡村派

树莓、草莓、柠檬和酸橙
我有什么好挑的?
蓝莓、苹果、樱桃、南瓜和李子
打电话约晚餐,亲爱的,我这就过来

给大白鹅备好鞍
把我绑在上面,撒开缰绳
天,天哪
我爱死了那个乡村派

我要的不多,我真不骗你
这又不是比赛

Give to me my country pie
I won't throw it up in anybody's face

Shake me up that old peach tree
Little Jack Horner's got nothin' on me
Oh me, oh my
Love that country pie

把我的乡村派给我
我不会吐到任何人脸上

把老桃树给我摇一摇
小杰克·霍纳[1]比不了
天,天哪
我爱死了那个乡村派

---

[1] 小杰克·霍纳,英语同名童谣中唱:小杰克·霍纳/坐在墙旮旯/吃着圣诞派。

TONIGHT I'LL BE STAYING HERE WITH YOU

Throw my ticket out the window
Throw my suitcase out there, too
Throw my troubles out the door
I don't need them anymore
'Cause tonight I'll be staying here with you

I should have left this town this morning
But it was more than I could do
Oh, your love comes on so strong
And I've waited all day long
For tonight when I'll be staying here with you

Is it really any wonder
The love that a stranger might receive
You cast your spell and I went under
I find it so difficult to leave

I can hear that whistle blowin'
I see that stationmaster, too
If there's a poor boy on the street
Then let him have my seat
'Cause tonight I'll be staying here with you

今夜我要在这儿陪你

把我的票丢出窗
把我的行李箱也扔出去
把我的烦恼抛至门外
这些都不需要了
因为今夜我要在这儿陪你

本来今早就该离开小城
可我实在走不动
啊,你的爱来得太猛
我等了一整天
就为了今夜能在这儿陪你

这很奇怪吗
一个异乡人得到的爱情
你下了咒语,我被它击中
发现要离开竟是如此不可能

我能听见汽笛声声
我也看到了那个站长
如果街上有个穷孩子
就把我的座位让给他吧
因为今夜我要在这儿陪你

Throw my ticket out the window

Throw my suitcase out there, too

Throw my troubles out the door

I don't need them anymore

'Cause tonight I'll be staying here with you

把我的票丢出窗
把我的行李箱也扔出去
把我的烦恼抛至门外
这些都不需要了
因为今夜我要在这儿陪你

WANTED MAN

Wanted man in California, wanted man in Buffalo
Wanted man in Kansas City, wanted man in Ohio
Wanted man in Mississippi, wanted man in old Cheyenne
Wherever you might look tonight, you might see this wanted man

I might be in Colorado or Georgia by the sea
Working for some man who may not know at all who I might be
If you ever see me comin' and if you know who I am
Don't you breathe it to nobody 'cause you know I'm on the lam

Wanted man by Lucy Watson, wanted man by Jeannie Brown
Wanted man by Nellie Johnson, wanted man in this next town
But I've had all that I've wanted of a lot of things I had
And a lot more than I needed of some things that turned out bad

I got sidetracked in El Paso, stopped to get myself a map
Went the wrong way into Juarez with Juanita on my lap
Then I went to sleep in Shreveport, woke up in Abilene
Wonderin' why the hell I'm wanted at some town halfway between

通缉犯

加州通缉犯,布法罗通缉犯
堪萨斯城通缉犯,俄亥俄州通缉犯
密西西比通缉犯,老夏延镇通缉犯
今晚无论朝哪儿看,你都可能会看到这个通缉犯

可能我在科罗拉多或海边的佐治亚
雇用我的人可能完全不知道我的底细
如果你见我走来,如果你认出了我是谁
别向任何人泄露,因为你知道我正在跑路

露西·沃森追的人,珍妮·布朗追的人
内莉·约翰逊追的人,下一个镇子追的人 [1]
但我已拥有了全部我想要的那许许多多
还包括更多超出我需要的、结果变坏的玩意儿

在埃尔帕索走岔了路,我停下来搞了张地图
腿上坐着胡安妮塔,走错路误入了华雷斯
然后在什里夫波特入睡,在阿比林醒来
真搞不懂为什么在半路的什么小镇我就成了通缉犯

---

[1] 通缉犯,wanted man,字面上又是"想要的人",这一段要缉捕他的都是女警,一语双关。

Wanted man in Albuquerque, wanted man in Syracuse
Wanted man in Tallahassee, wanted man in Baton Rouge
There's somebody set to grab me anywhere that I might be
And wherever you might look tonight, you might get a glimpse of me

Wanted man in California, wanted man in Buffalo
Wanted man in Kansas City, wanted man in Ohio
Wanted man in Mississippi, wanted man in old Cheyenne
Wherever you might look tonight, you might see this wanted man

阿尔伯克基通缉犯,锡拉丘兹通缉犯
塔拉哈西通缉犯,巴吞鲁日通缉犯
不管我去哪儿,总有人准备要抓我
今晚无论朝哪儿看,你都可能会瞧见我呢

加州通缉犯,布法罗通缉犯
堪萨斯城通缉犯,俄亥俄州通缉犯
密西西比通缉犯,老夏延镇通缉犯
今晚无论朝哪儿看,你都可能会看到这个通缉犯

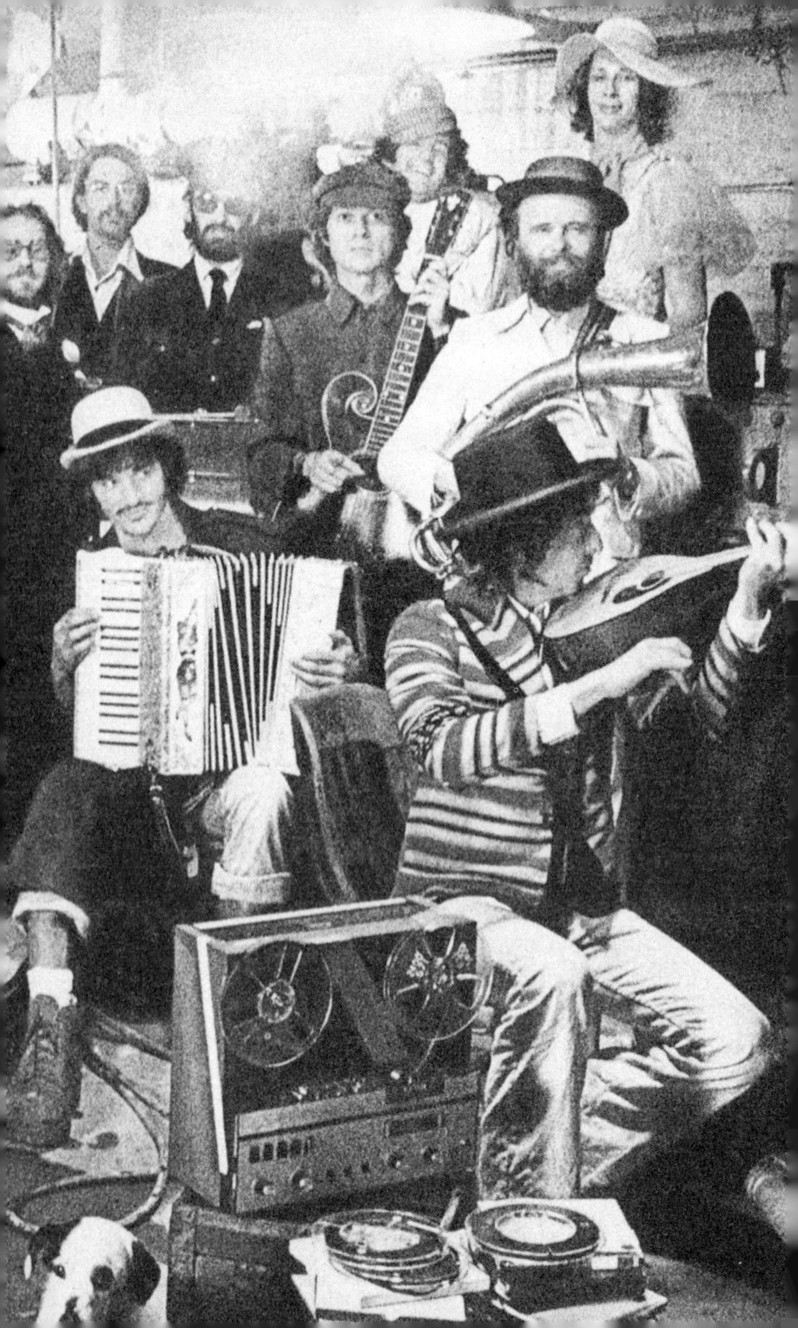

THE BASEMENT TAPES
地下室录音带

鸡零狗碎

百万美元狂欢

去阿卡普尔科

看哪!

晾衣绳传奇

小苹果树

求你啦,亨利太太

愤怒的泪水

太多虚无

是啊!很重而且还有一瓶面包

坠入洪流

小蒙哥马利

哪儿都不去

不要告诉亨利

还什么都未交付

开门,荷马

长途接线员

这车轮烧起来了

附加歌词

十字架上的名号
爱斯基摩人魁恩(威猛魁恩)
我将获得自由

把你的石头拿开!
不说话的周末
圣菲

like a poor fool in his prime/trying to read your portrait
you can hear me talk

  is your heart made of stone/
                        or solid rock?

got fourteen fevers and five believers all dressed up ~~fiiiiii~~ *so fine*
tell your mama and poppa not to worry cause theyre friends of mine

dressed up like men

《地下室录音带》诞生于1967年，与专辑《约翰·韦斯利·哈丁》同时，却直到8年后才由哥伦比亚唱片公司于1975年6月26日发行，成为迪伦的第16张录音室专辑。本来，这些歌曲也没打算发行，只是迪伦与"乐队"的即兴之作，以专业录音师个人自制的方式录制。

对流行音乐史来说，美国民歌秘史自此掀开一角，日后的独立制作、另类乡村等潮流，都从这里发源。

1966年7月29日早上，迪伦驾驶摩托车在伍德斯托克附近的小村庄侧滑翻车。车祸让他从鬼门关走了一遭，也让他从仿佛有千钧重量的人生压力下解脱出来。

在康复期间，迪伦读了许多书，有的来自"你从未听过的作者"（迪伦语）。许多朋友看到，一本巨大的《圣经》放在他起居室中间的高台上，旁边是汉克·威廉姆斯（Hank Williams）的歌词集。

同年，"乐队"在伍德斯托克租下了一栋乡村楼房，因其外立面为粉红色而被称为"大粉红"，地下室改造成了乐队成员的住所和排练室。

1967年，迪伦时常造访"大粉红"，与"乐队"一起玩音乐、录音。高峰时，他一周来三四次，一周能写10首歌。一半是玩儿，一半是为威特马克父子唱片公司提供歌曲和样带，迪伦和"乐队"录了100多首歌。他们将其中14首制成了录音带，赠送给临近的音乐家朋友，"地下室录音带"由此流传到了公众层面。

1975年，哥伦比亚唱片公司公开发行《地下室录音带》，内含18首迪伦歌曲和8首"乐队"歌曲。随着时间的推移，越来越多的"地下室录音带"歌曲浮出水面。规模最大的"完整版"，于2014年11月4日由哥伦比亚唱片公司发行，以《靴子腿系列·第11卷》(*The Bootleg Series Vol.11*)为名，收录了1967年6月到10月迪伦和"乐队"的138首曲目，共计6张唱片，其中有些歌曲录了不止一个版本。

"地下室录音带"歌曲有着特殊的质地和光彩。迪伦研究专家、音乐历史学家格雷尔·马库斯曾以《老美国志异》为名，写了整整一本书来评论这些歌，他说：

"这张专辑仿佛位于忏悔室与妓院之间。它的音乐带来一种熟悉的光环，或者是某种口口相传、不见经传的传统，以及一种自我认识的深刻感觉……它们既富于历史意义，同时又自成机杼。音乐是有趣而令人感到安慰的；与此同时又显得有些奇异，有种未完成的感觉。

"这些东西听上去像是一种本能的实验，抑或一个神秘的实验室，这实验室成为美国文化语言复苏与再创造的矿床。

"如果把这些录音标上1881、1932、1967、1954、1992……诸如此类，随便什么年代，它们也同样会令听者信服。"[1]

---

[1] 格雷尔·马库斯.老美国志异[M].董楠,译.南京：南京大学出版社，2008.

"乐队"吉他手、词曲作家罗比·罗伯逊（Robbie Robertson）说："他（迪伦）并不想公开发表这些歌，我们都不知道这些歌是他创作出来的，还是他脑海里本来就有的。"

该怎样理解马库斯的评论，以及收入在本书中的这24首作品呢？

以我之见，可以这样理解。

在美国民歌乃至英语民歌历史上，深埋着一口黑暗的井，其中不乏在信息透明的今天看起来是令人费解、晦涩、幽暗乃至神秘的歌曲。它们有些是讲述奇案，有些是关于怪人，有些属于异事，因此成为民歌库存中隐秘的部分。迪伦以其为源泉，加入私密的个人动机，联系上现实图景、时代动荡、美国记忆、民族心理，在完全放松和自由的状态下，改造和重写传统，录制出了这一系列具有与古老英语民歌同样品质的歌曲。比如有人指出，《百万美元狂欢》写的是安迪·沃霍尔的"工厂"晚会；《晾衣绳传奇》戏仿了当年的民歌金曲，该曲讲述一个年轻人自杀以及他隐秘的情史；《愤怒的泪水》可以理解为对越战、对美国国家认同的破灭；《太多虚无》是对 T. S. 艾略特的议论，表达了迪伦对他不负责任的私生活的不满……总之，这些歌曲是狂欢式的、乱来的、装疯卖傻的，又是闹剧、祭典、寓言和民间启示录。

收录在这里的这24首，包括1975年《地下室录音带》专辑中迪伦创作的18首，以及散落在其他出版物中的另外6首。

ODDS AND ENDS

I plan it all and I take my place
You break your promise all over the place
You promised to love me, but what do I see
Just you comin' and spillin' juice over me
Odds and ends, odds and ends
Lost time is not found again

Now, you take your file and you bend my head
I never can remember anything that you said
You promised to love me, but what do I know
You're always spillin' juice on me like you got someplace to go
Odds and ends, odds and ends
Lost time is not found again

Now, I've had enough, my box is clean
You know what I'm sayin' and you know what I mean
From now on you'd best get on someone else

鸡零狗碎 [1]

我计划好了一切并已经到位
你却处处违背诺言
你信誓旦旦说爱我,可我看到了什么
看到你过来泼我一身果汁
鸡零狗碎,鸡零狗碎
失去的时光找不回

现在,你拿来账本压我低头
你说的一切我都不记得
你信誓旦旦说爱我,可我明白了什么
明白你总是泼我一身果汁,像是你有地方要去
鸡零狗碎,鸡零狗碎
失去的时光找不回

现在我受够了,清空了箱底
你知道我在说什么,你也明白我的意思
从现在起你最好找别人去

---

[1] 英国评论家迈克尔·格雷(Michael Gray)指出:这首歌与美国布鲁斯歌手吉米·里德(Jimmy Reed)1957年录制的一首歌同名;它听上去有巴迪·霍利(Buddy Holly)歌曲的旨趣和味道。这首及《地下室录音带》专辑的全部篇目,均系郝佳校译。

While you're doin' it, keep that juice to yourself

Odds and ends, odds and ends

Lost time is not found again

真这么做时,把果汁留给你自己吧
鸡零狗碎,鸡零狗碎
失去的时光找不回

MILLION DOLLAR BASH

Well, that big dumb blonde
With her wheel in the gorge
And Turtle, that friend of theirs
With his checks all forged
And his cheeks in a chunk
With his cheese in the cash
They're all gonna be there
At that million dollar bash
Ooh, baby, ooh-ee
Ooh, baby, ooh-ee
It's that million dollar bash

Ev'rybody from right now
To over there and back
The louder they come
The harder they crack
Come now, sweet cream
Don't forget to flash
We're all gonna meet
At that million dollar bash
Ooh, baby, ooh-ee
Ooh, baby, ooh-ee

百万美元狂欢

哦,那傻大个儿金发妹
方向盘卡在乳沟
而"乌龟",他们的朋友
支票全是假的
脸上堆满肉
钞票上尽是他的奶酪
他们全都将抵达
那百万美元狂欢
噢,宝贝,噢嘿
噢,宝贝,噢嘿
那可是百万美元狂欢

从现在起每个人
都要去那边再回来
来时越喧哗的
垮得越厉害
来吧,甜奶油
别忘记拍照
我们都会团聚
在那百万美元狂欢
噢,宝贝,噢嘿
噢,宝贝,噢嘿

It's that million dollar bash

Well, I took my counselor
Out to the barn
Silly Nelly was there
She told him a yarn
Then along came Jones
Emptied the trash
Ev'rybody went down
To that million dollar bash
Ooh, baby, ooh-ee
Ooh, baby, ooh-ee
It's that million dollar bash

Well, I'm hittin' it too hard
My stones won't take
I get up in the mornin'
But it's too early to wake
First it's hello, goodbye
Then push and then crash
But we're all gonna make it
At that million dollar bash

那可是百万美元狂欢

哦,我带了律师
去大仓房
蠢货内莉在那儿
她给他讲了个段子
然后琼斯来了 [1]
清空了垃圾
人人都前往
去那百万美元狂欢
噢,宝贝,噢嘿
噢,宝贝,噢嘿
那可是百万美元狂欢

哦,我撞得太狠了
我的石头 [2] 受不住
我早上起来
但是太早了,还没清醒
先是你好,再见
然后推再然后撞
我们都会挺过去
在那百万美元狂欢

---

[1] "琼斯来了"源于贸易船乐队(The Coasters)的歌名,该乐队另一首歌《喋喋不休》("Yakety Yak")中提到"带走那些纸和垃圾"。
[2] stones,俚语有睾丸、胆量之意。

Ooh, baby, ooh-ee
Ooh, baby, ooh-ee
It's that million dollar bash

Well, I looked at my watch
I looked at my wrist
Punched myself in the face
With my fist
I took my potatoes
Down to be mashed
Then I made it over
To that million dollar bash
Ooh, baby, ooh-ee
Ooh, baby, ooh-ee
It's that million dollar bash

噢，宝贝，噢嘿
噢，宝贝，噢嘿
那可是百万美元狂欢

哦，我看了看手表
看了看我的手腕
往自己脸上
砸了一拳
我拿起了马铃薯
拿去捣成泥
再转送到
那百万美元狂欢上
噢，宝贝，噢嘿
噢，宝贝，噢嘿
那可是百万美元狂欢

GOIN' TO ACAPULCO

I'm going down to Rose Marie's
She never does me wrong
She puts it to me plain as day
And gives it to me for a song

It's a wicked life but what the hell
The stars ain't falling down
I'm standing outside the Taj Mahal
I don't see no one around

Goin' to Acapulco—goin' on the run
Goin' down to see fat gut—goin' to have some fun
Yeah—goin' to have some fun

Now, whenever I get up
And I ain't got what I see
I just make it down to Rose Marie's
'Bout a quarter after three

There are worse ways of getting there

去阿卡普尔科 [1]

我要去罗斯·玛丽那儿
她待我一直不错
跟我就像大白天般直白
唱一支歌她就给我

生活很操蛋,但那又怎么样
星星不会掉到地上
我站在泰姬陵的外面
一个人影子都没看见

去阿卡普尔科——继续在路上
去看看大肚腩——好好玩它一场
呀——好好玩它一场

现在,不管我何时起床
我都搞不懂我看到的
我就在三点一刻左右
去罗斯·玛丽那儿

去那儿的路不好走

---

[1] 阿卡普尔科,墨西哥南部港口城市。

And I ain't complainin' none
If the clouds don't drop and the train don't stop
I'm bound to meet the sun

Goin' to Acapulco—goin' on the run
Goin' down to see fat gut—goin' to have some fun
Yeah—goin' to have some fun

Now, if someone offers me a joke
I just say no thanks
I try to tell it like it is
And keep away from pranks

Well, sometime you know when the well breaks down
I just go pump on it some
Rose Marie, she likes to go to big places
And just set there waitin' for me to come

Goin' to Acapulco—goin' on the run
Goin' down to see fat gut—goin' to have some fun
Yeah—goin' to have some fun

但是我一点儿不抱怨
如果云彩不落而火车不停
我就注定会与太阳见面

去阿卡普尔科——继续在路上
去看看大肚腩——好好玩它一场
呀——好好玩它一场

现在，若有谁跟我开玩笑
我只是说不了谢谢
我试着照原样讲
由此远离恶作剧

哦，你知道有时井不出水
我就去压它那么几下
罗斯·玛丽，她喜欢去大地方
她会在那儿准备好，等着我到来

去阿卡普尔科——继续在路上
去看看大肚腩——好好玩它一场
呀——好好玩它一场

LO AND BEHOLD!

I pulled out for San Anton'
I never felt so good
My woman said she'd meet me there
And of course, I knew she would
The coachman, he hit me for my hook
And he asked me my name
I give it to him right away
Then I hung my head in shame
Lo and behold! Lo and behold!
Lookin' for my lo and behold
Get me outa here, my dear man!

I come into Pittsburgh
At six-thirty flat
I found myself a vacant seat
An' I put down my hat
"What's the matter, Molly, dear
What's the matter with your mound?"
"What's it to ya, Moby Dick?

看哪!

我出发去圣安东
从没感觉有这么好
我的女人说她会在那儿见我
当然,我知道她会
那个列车员,为了我的搭讪给了我一下
他问我叫什么名儿
我立刻告诉了他
然后羞愧地垂下头
看哪!看哪!
寻找我的"看哪"
我的好老弟,快带我离开这里!

我到了匹兹堡
刚好六点三十
给自己找了个空位
然后,我摘下帽子
"怎么了,莫莉亲爱的
你的土丘出了什么问题?"
"这跟你有何相干,大白鲸[1]?

---

[1] 大白鲸,梅尔维尔小说《白鲸》中的鲸鱼,在俗语中引申为男人下体。

This is chicken town!"
Lo and behold! Lo and behold!
Lookin' for my lo and behold
Get me outa here, my dear man!

I bought my girl
A herd of moose
One she could call her own
Well, she came out the very next day
To see where they had flown
I'm goin' down to Tennessee
Get me a truck 'r somethin'
Gonna save my money and rip it up!
Lo and behold! Lo and behold!
Lookin' for my lo and behold
Get me outa here, my dear man!

Now, I come in on a Ferris wheel
An' boys, I sure was slick
I come in like a ton of bricks
Laid a few tricks on 'em
Goin' back to Pittsburgh

这里是鸡崽城 [1]！"
看哪！看哪！
寻找我的"看哪"
我的好老弟，快带我离开这里！

我给我的女朋友
买了一大群麋鹿
她可以说这都是她自己的
好吧，第二天她出来看
它们都跑哪儿去了
我要去田纳西
找个卡车司机的活儿 [2]
攒点儿钱，再把它们都撕碎！
看哪！看哪！
寻找我的"看哪"
我的好老弟，快带我离开这里！

现在，我坐着摩天轮进来了
伙计们，我肯定很老油条
我像一吨砖头一样进来了
对他们要上几个小把戏
回匹兹堡去

---

[1] 文字游戏，"这里是鸡崽城"双关"这里都是胆小鬼"。
[2] "我要去田纳西／找个卡车司机的活儿"，据迈克尔·格雷说，此处指涉"猫王"，他成名前在田纳西州当卡车司机。

Count up to thirty
Round that horn and ride that herd
Gonna thread up!
Lo and behold! Lo and behold!
Lookin' for my lo and behold
Get me outa here, my dear man!

数到三十
绕过那只角,跨上鹿群
挽轭成列!
看哪!看哪!
寻找我的"看哪"
我的好老弟,快带我离开这里!

CLOTHES LINE SAGA

After a while we took in the clothes
Nobody said very much
Just some old wild shirts and a couple pairs of pants
Which nobody really wanted to touch
Mama come in and picked up a book
An' Papa asked her what it was
Someone else asked, "What do you care?"
Papa said, "Well, just because"
Then they started to take back their clothes
Hang 'em on the line
It was January the thirtieth
And everybody was feelin' fine

The next day everybody got up
Seein' if the clothes were dry
The dogs were barking, a neighbor passed
Mama, of course, she said, "Hi!"
"Have you heard the news?" he said, with a grin

晾衣绳传奇 [1]

稍后我们收进衣服
谁都没多说什么
只是几件皱巴巴的旧衬衣和两条裤子
没有人真的想碰
妈妈进来拿起一本书
爸爸问她是什么
有人说:"关你什么事?"
爸爸说:"这个,不为什么"
然后他们开始取回衣服
挂到绳子上
这是一月三十号
人人都感觉不错

第二天大家起来
看衣服干了没有
狗在叫,一个邻居经过
妈妈,当然她说:"嗨!"
"你听了新闻吗?"他问,咧开嘴

---

[1] 这首歌原名《对〈颂歌〉的应答》("Answer to 'Ode'"),克林顿·海林认为它是对美国民谣歌手鲍比·金特里(Bobbie Gentry)的歌曲《比利·乔颂歌》("Ode to Billie Joe")的戏仿。

"The Vice-President's gone mad!"

"Where?" "Downtown." "When?" "Last night"

"Hmm, say, that's too bad!"

"Well, there's nothin' we can do about it," said the neighbor

"It's just somethin' we're gonna have to forget"

"Yes, I guess so," said Ma

Then she asked me if the clothes was still wet

I reached up, touched my shirt

And the neighbor said, "Are those clothes yours?"

I said, "Some of 'em, not all of 'em"

He said, "Ya always help out around here with the chores?"

I said, "Sometime, not all the time"

Then my neighbor, he blew his nose

Just as Papa yelled outside

"Mama wants you t' come back in the house and bring them clothes"

Well, I just do what I'm told

So, I did it, of course

I went back in the house and Mama met me

And then I shut all the doors

"副总统疯了!"
"在哪儿?""城里。""什么时候?""昨晚"
"嗯,啧啧,这可真糟!"
"嘻,我们对此无能为力,"邻居说
"不过是些我们得忘掉的事"
"是的,我想也是。"妈妈说
然后她问我衣服是不是还没干

我伸手摸摸我的衬衫
邻居问:"这些衣服是你的?"
我说:"有些是,不全是"
他说:"你总在帮忙干这些杂事?"
我说:"有时候,不是所有时候"
然后邻居,擤起了鼻涕
这时候爸爸在外面喊
"妈妈叫你把衣服给他们
　拿进屋"
哦,我只是听令行事
所以,我当然,这样做了
我进了屋,妈妈迎着我
然后我关上所有的门

APPLE SUCKLING TREE

Old man sailin' in a dinghy boat

Down there

Old man down is baitin' a hook

On there

Gonna pull man down on a suckling hook

Gonna pull man into the suckling brook

Oh yeah!

Now, he's underneath that apple suckling tree

Oh yeah!

Under that apple suckling tree

Oh yeah!

That's underneath that tree

There's gonna be just you and me

Underneath that apple suckling tree

Oh yeah!

I push him back and I stand in line

Oh yeah!

小苹果树 [1]

老人划着小划子
去那儿
老人给鱼钩上了饵
在那儿
马上小小鱼钩要把人拉下去
马上要把人拉下小溪
噢,对!

这会儿,他在那棵小苹果树底下
噢,对!
在那棵小苹果树下
噢,对!
在那棵树底下
将只有你和我
在那棵小苹果树底下
噢,对!

我推他回去然后我排队等着
噢,对!

---

[1] 美国当代著名乐评人格雷尔·马库斯指出,这首歌的曲调源自古老的童谣《青蛙去求婚》("Froggy Went A-Courtin'")。

Then I hush my Sadie and stand in line
Oh yeah!
Then I hush my Sadie and stand in line
I get on board in two-eyed time
Oh yeah!

Under that apple suckling tree
Oh yeah!
Under that apple suckling tree
Oh yeah!
Underneath that tree
There's just gonna be you and me
Underneath that apple suckling tree
Oh yeah!

Now, who's on the table, who's to tell me?
Oh yeah!
Who's on the table, who's to tell me?
Oh yeah!
Who should I tell, oh, who should I tell?
The forty-nine of you like bats out of hell
Oh underneath that old apple suckling tree

然后我让我的萨迪静下来我排队等着
噢,对!
然后我让我的萨迪静下来我排队等着
两眼一眨的工夫我上了船
噢,对!

在那棵小苹果树下
噢,对!
在那棵小苹果树下
噢,对!
在那棵树底下
就将会有你和我
在那棵小苹果树底下
噢,对!

这会儿,谁在桌上,谁来告诉我?
噢,对!
谁在桌上,谁来告诉我?
噢,对!
我该告诉谁,啊,我该告诉谁?
你们四十九个,像地狱里飞出的蝙蝠
啊,在那棵古老的小苹果树底下

PLEASE, MRS. HENRY

Well, I've already had two beers
I'm ready for the broom
Please, Missus Henry, won't you
Take me to my room?
I'm a good ol' boy
But I've been sniffin' too many eggs
Talkin' to too many people
Drinkin' too many kegs
Please, Missus Henry, Missus Henry, please!
Please, Missus Henry, Missus Henry, please!
I'm down on my knees
An' I ain't got a dime

Well, I'm groanin' in a hallway
Pretty soon I'll be mad
Please, Missus Henry, won't you
Take me to your dad?
I can drink like a fish
I can crawl like a snake
I can bite like a turkey
I can slam like a drake
Please, Missus Henry, Missus Henry, please!

求你啦,亨利太太

哦,我喝了两扎啤酒
准备好被扫出去
求你啦,亨利太太你能不能
带我去我的屋?
我是个好小伙儿
但是我吸了太多蛋
跟太多人说话
灌了太多黄汤
求你啦,亨利太太,亨利太太,求求你!
求你啦,亨利太太,亨利太太,求求你!
我现在跪下啦
我一个子儿都没啦

哦,我在门厅里呻吟
再过不一会儿我要疯了
求你啦,亨利太太你能不能
带我去见你爹?
我能像鱼那样喝
像蛇那样爬
像火鸡那样咬
像鸭子那样啄
求你啦,亨利太太,亨利太太,求求你!

Please, Missus Henry, Missus Henry, please!
I'm down on my knees
An' I ain't got a dime

Now, don't crowd me, lady
Or I'll fill up your shoe
I'm a sweet bourbon daddy
An' tonight I am blue
I'm a thousand years old
And I'm a generous bomb
I'm T-boned and punctured
But I'm known to be calm
Please, Missus Henry, Missus Henry, please!
Please, Missus Henry, Missus Henry, please!
I'm down on my knees
An' I ain't got a dime

Now, I'm startin' to drain
My stool's gonna squeak
If I walk too much farther
My crane's gonna leak
Look, Missus Henry
There's only so much I can do
Why don't you look my way

求你啦,亨利太太,亨利太太,求求你!
我现在跪下啦
我一个子儿都没啦

好啦,别推我了女士
不然我会灌你一鞋
我是可爱的波旁[1]老爹
今天晚上很忧郁
我已经一千岁了
是颗慷慨的炸弹
生有丁字骨并且穿了孔
但大家都知道我是个冷静的人
求你啦,亨利太太,亨利太太,求求你!
求你啦,亨利太太,亨利太太,求求你!
我现在跪下啦
我一个子儿都没啦

现在,我得去排排涝了
我的凳子要吱吱叫了
要是走太远
我的起重机要漏水了
看,亨利太太
我能做的不过就这些
为什么你不从我的角度看

---

[1] 波旁,即波本威士忌。

An' pump me a few?

Please, Missus Henry, Missus Henry, please!

Please, Missus Henry, Missus Henry, please!

I'm down on my knees

An' I ain't got a dime

再帮我满上几杯?
求你啦,亨利太太,亨利太太,求求你!
求你啦,亨利太太,亨利太太,求求你!
我现在跪下啦
我一个子儿都没啦

TEARS OF RAGE
(WITH RICHARD MANUEL)

We carried you in our arms

On Independence Day

And now you'd throw us all aside

And put us on our way

Oh what dear daughter 'neath the sun

Would treat a father so

To wait upon him hand and foot

And always tell him, "No"?

Tears of rage, tears of grief

Why must I always be the thief?

Come to me now, you know

We're so alone

And life is brief

We pointed out the way to go

And scratched your name in sand

Though you just thought it was nothing more

愤怒的泪水 [1]

（与理查德·曼纽尔合作）

我们用我们的手臂抱着你
在独立日
可是现在，你把我们扔到了一边儿
让我们自寻出路
噢，天底下什么样的亲闺女
会这样对待父亲
无微不至地伺候他
又总是对他说"不"？
愤怒的泪水，悲伤的泪水
为什么总是要我做贼？
来我这儿吧，你知道
我们是如此孤单
而人生短暂

我们指出了要走的路
在沙地上划你的名字
然而你觉得这不过是

---

[1] 英国评论家安迪·吉尔（Andy Gill）将这首歌比作李尔王（莎士比亚戏剧《李尔王》主角）在荒野的悲愤独白，并将这种悲愤与1967年越南战争扩大时的美国社会分裂现象联系了起来。

Than a place for you to stand
Now, I want you to know that while we watched
You discover there was no one true
Most ev'rybody really thought
It was a childish thing to do
Tears of rage, tears of grief
Must I always be the thief?
Come to me now, you know
We're so low
And life is brief

It was all very painless
When you went out to receive
All that false instruction
Which we never could believe
And now the heart is filled with gold
As if it was a purse
But, oh, what kind of love is this
Which goes from bad to worse?
Tears of rage, tears of grief
Must I always be the thief?
Come to me now, you know
We're so low
And life is brief

让你有了立足之地
现在我要你明白，当我们照看你时
你发现无人出于真心
大多数人真的认为
做这件事实在幼稚
愤怒的泪水，悲伤的泪水
难道总是要我做贼？
来我这儿吧，你知道
我们是如此低贱
而人生短暂

这本来毫无痛苦
当你出去接受那些
我们永远不会信的
错误信条
可是现在，这心里装满了金子
仿佛它是只钱包
但是，哦，这是种什么爱
从坏变得更坏？
愤怒的泪水，悲伤的泪水
难道总是要我做贼？
来我这儿吧，你知道
我们是如此低贱
而人生短暂

TOO MUCH OF NOTHING

Now, too much of nothing
Can make a man feel ill at ease
One man's temper might rise
While another man's temper might freeze
In the day of confession
We cannot mock a soul
Oh, when there's too much of nothing
No one has control

Say hello to Valerie
Say hello to Vivian
Send them all my salary
On the waters of oblivion

Too much of nothing
Can make a man abuse a king
He can walk the streets and boast like most
But he wouldn't know a thing
Now, it's all been done before

太多虚无

现在,太多虚无
会让人感到不自在
可能一个人的脾气上来了
而另一个人的脾气结成了冰
忏悔的日子
我们不能嘲弄灵魂
啊,当有太多虚无
谁都无法控制

向瓦莱丽问好
向薇薇安[1]问好
给她们我所有的薪水
在遗忘河上

太多虚无
会让人辱骂君王[2]
他可以上街,像大多数人一样吹牛
但是他什么都不明白
哦,这一切都已发生过

---

[1] 瓦莱丽和薇薇安是英国诗人 T. S. 艾略特两任妻子的名字。
[2] "会让人辱骂君王",《旧约·传道书》10:20:"你不可咒诅君王……"

It's all been written in the book
But when there's too much of nothing
Nobody should look

Say hello to Valerie
Say hello to Vivian
Send them all my salary
On the waters of oblivion

Too much of nothing
Can turn a man into a liar
It can cause one man to sleep on nails
And another man to eat fire
Ev'rybody's doin' somethin'
I heard it in a dream
But when there's too much of nothing
It just makes a fella mean

Say hello to Valerie
Say hello to Vivian
Send them all my salary
On the waters of oblivion

这一切都写入了那本书
可是，因为有太多虚无
没有人会去看

向瓦莱丽问好
向薇薇安问好
给她们我所有的薪水
在遗忘河上

太多虚无
会让人变成骗子
会让一个人睡钉板
而另一个人吞食火焰
每个人都在做些什么
我在梦中听到这些
可是，就因为有太多虚无
让好小伙儿变得卑劣

向瓦莱丽问好
向薇薇安问好
给她们我所有的薪水
在遗忘河上

YEA! HEAVY AND A BOTTLE OF BREAD

Well, the comic book and me, just us, we caught the bus
The poor little chauffeur, though, she was back in bed
On the very next day, with a nose full of pus
Yea! Heavy and a bottle of bread
Yea! Heavy and a bottle of bread
Yea! Heavy and a bottle of bread

It's a one-track town, just brown, and a breeze, too
Pack up the meat, sweet, we're headin' out
For Wichita in a pile of fruit
Get the loot, don't be slow, we're gonna catch a trout
Get the loot, don't be slow, we're gonna catch a trout
Get the loot, don't be slow, we're gonna catch a trout

Now, pull that drummer out from behind that bottle
Bring me my pipe, we're gonna shake it
Slap that drummer with a pie that smells
Take me down to California, baby
Take me down to California, baby
Take me down to California, baby

是啊!很重而且还有一瓶面包

哦,漫画书和我,就我们俩,赶上了公交车
但可怜的小司机,她回床去睡觉
就在第二天,鼻子里满是浓鼻涕
是啊!很重而且还有一瓶面包
是啊!很重而且还有一瓶面包
是啊!很重而且还有一瓶面包

这是一条道的城,只有棕色,还有微风
包起肉,宝贝儿,我们要出门
向水果堆里的威奇托[1]进发
去夺战利品,动作快点,我们去弄条鳟鱼
去夺战利品,动作快点,我们去弄条鳟鱼
去夺战利品,动作快点,我们去弄条鳟鱼

现在,把那鼓手从瓶子后面拖出来
把我的烟斗拿来,我们要去摇一摇
用变味儿的派拍那位鼓手
带我去加利福尼亚,亲爱的
带我去加利福尼亚,亲爱的
带我去加利福尼亚,亲爱的

---

[1] 威奇托,美国堪萨斯州南部城市。

Yes, the comic book and me, just us, we caught the bus
The poor little chauffeur, though, she was back in bed
On the very next day, with a nose full of pus
Yea! Heavy and a bottle of bread
Yea! Heavy and a bottle of bread
Yea! Heavy and a bottle of bread

是的,漫画书和我,就我们俩,赶上了公交车
但可怜的小司机,她回床去睡觉
第二天,鼻子里满是浓鼻涕
是啊!很重而且还有一瓶面包
是啊!很重而且还有一瓶面包
是啊!很重而且还有一瓶面包

DOWN IN THE FLOOD

Crash on the levee, mama

Water's gonna overflow

Swamp's gonna rise

No boat's gonna row

Now, you can train on down

To Williams Point

You can bust your feet

You can rock this joint

But oh mama, ain't you gonna miss your best friend now?

You're gonna have to find yourself

Another best friend, somehow

Now, don't you try an' move me

You're just gonna lose

There's a crash on the levee

And, mama, you've been refused

Well, it's sugar for sugar

And salt for salt

If you go down in the flood

坠入洪流

大堤决口了,妈妈
洪水就要泛滥
沼泽将扩大
将没有船能够航行
现在,你可以乘火车
去威廉斯角 [1]
你可以踏破脚
可以在酒吧胡闹
可是啊妈妈,这时你不会想念你的至交吗?
你的至交
你得为自己另找一个,无论如何

现在,别想来说服我
你只会失去
大堤破了道口子
而妈妈,你已遭到拒绝
瞧,这就是以糖还糖
以盐还盐
如果你坠入洪流

---

[1] 威廉斯角,位于南极洲南设得兰群岛的海岬。

It's gonna be your own fault
Oh mama, ain't you gonna miss your best friend now?
You're gonna have to find yourself
Another best friend, somehow

Well, that high tide's risin'
Mama, don't you let me down
Pack up your suitcase
Mama, don't you make a sound
Now, it's king for king
Queen for queen
It's gonna be the meanest flood
That anybody's seen
Oh mama, ain't you gonna miss your best friend now?
Yes, you're gonna have to find yourself
Another best friend, somehow

这将是你自己的错 [1]

啊妈妈,这时你不会想念你的至交吗?

你的至交

你得为自己另找一个,无论如何

哦,洪峰还在上涨

妈妈,你不要叫我失望

去收拾行李吧

妈妈,不要声张

瞧,这就是以后还后

以王还王

这会是一场,所有人见过的

最无情的洪水

啊妈妈,这时你不会想念你的至交吗?

你的至交

是的,你得为自己另找一个,无论如何

---

[1] "瞧,这就是以糖还糖/以盐还盐/如果你坠入洪流/这将是你自己的错"——迈克尔·格雷指出,此处改编自美国蓝调歌手"兔子"布朗(Rabbit Brown)的《詹姆斯巷蓝调》("James Alley Blues");"我会对你以糖还糖,让你以盐还盐/要是你跟我处不来,那是你自己的错"。

TINY MONTGOMERY

Well you can tell ev'rybody
Down in ol' Frisco
Tell 'em
Tiny Montgomery says hello

Now ev'ry boy and girl's
Gonna get their bang
'Cause Tiny Montgomery's
Gonna shake that thing
Tell ev'rybody
Down in ol' Frisco
That Tiny Montgomery's comin'
Down to say hello

Skinny Moo and
Half-track Frank
They're gonna both be gettin'
Outa the tank
One bird book
And a buzzard and a crow
Tell 'em all
That Tiny's gonna say hello

小蒙哥马利

哦你可以告诉大家
在老旧金山
告诉他们
小蒙哥马利前来问候

马上每个男孩女孩
都会得到大惊喜
因为小蒙哥马利
将会摇起那个东西
去告诉大家
在老旧金山
小蒙哥马利来了
来问候

"瘦哞哞"和
"半履带"弗兰克
他们俩会
爬出舱来
独鸟书
还有秃鹰和乌鸦
告诉他们各位
小蒙哥马利要来问候

Scratch your dad

Do that bird

Suck that pig

And bring it on home

Pick that drip

And bake that dough

Tell 'em all

That Tiny says hello

Now he's king of the drunks

An' he squeezes, too

Watch out, Lester

Take it, Lou

Join the monks

The C.I.O.

Tell 'em all

That Tiny Montgomery says hello

Now grease that pig

And sing praise

Go on out

And gas that dog

Trick on in

挠你爹

做那鸟

舔那猪

并带回家

捡起水滴

烤那个面团

告诉他们各位

小蒙哥马利前来问候

现在他是醉汉之王

而且他也在挤

当心了莱斯特

拿着，卢

加入僧侣

产联 [1]

告诉他们各位

小蒙哥马利前来问候

现在给猪抹油

并且唱赞歌

跑出去

给那条小狗加气

捉弄捉弄

---

[1] 产联，即美国产业工人联合会。

Honk that stink
Take it on down
And watch it grow
Play it low
And pick it up
Take it on in
In a plucking cup
Three-legged man
And a hot-lipped hoe
Tell 'em all
Montgomery says hello

Well you can tell ev'rybody
Down in ol' Frisco
Tell 'em all
Montgomery says hello

按出臭味儿
拿下来
看它长
放低点
再抬高
把它装进
采集杯
三腿人
还有烈唇锄
告诉他们各位
蒙哥马利前来问候

哦你可以告诉大家
在老旧金山
告诉他们各位
蒙哥马利前来问候

YOU AIN'T GOIN' NOWHERE

Clouds so swift

Rain won't lift

Gate won't close

Railings froze

Get your mind off wintertime

You ain't goin' nowhere

Whoo-ee! Ride me high

Tomorrow's the day

My bride's gonna come

Oh, oh, are we gonna fly

Down in the easy chair!

I don't care

How many letters they sent

Morning came and morning went

Pick up your money

And pack up your tent

You ain't goin' nowhere

Whoo-ee! Ride me high

Tomorrow's the day

My bride's gonna come

Oh, oh, are we gonna fly

哪儿都不去

云飞动
雨未消
门不关
栅栏冻结
让思绪远离冬天
哪儿都不去
呜喂！骑着我嗨吧
明天就是大日子
我的新娘会到
噢，噢，我们会飞吗
就在这安乐椅上！

我才不管
他们发了多少信
早晨来了又去
拿好你的钱
收拾好帐篷
哪儿都不去
呜喂！骑着我嗨吧
明天就是大日子
我的新娘会到
噢，噢，我们会飞吗

Down in the easy chair!

Buy me a flute
And a gun that shoots
Tailgates and substitutes
Strap yourself
To the tree with roots
You ain't goin' nowhere
Whoo-ee! Ride me high
Tomorrow's the day
My bride's gonna come
Oh, oh, are we gonna fly
Down in the easy chair!

Genghis Khan
He could not keep
All his kings
Supplied with sleep
We'll climb that hill no matter how steep
When we get up to it
Whoo-ee! Ride me high
Tomorrow's the day
My bride's gonna come
Oh, oh, are we gonna fly
Down in the easy chair!

就在这安乐椅上!

给我买支长笛
再来把会射的枪
车挡板和代用品
系好安全带
在那棵扎着根儿的树上
哪儿都不去
呜喂!骑着我嗨吧
明天就是大日子
我的新娘会到
噢,噢,我们会飞吗
就在这安乐椅上!

成吉思汗
保不住他
所有的王
补充好睡眠
我们会爬上那山冈,不管多陡
等我们爬上去
呜喂!骑着我嗨吧
明天就是大日子
我的新娘会到
噢,噢,我们会飞吗
就在这安乐椅上!

DON'T YA TELL HENRY

Don't ya tell Henry
Apple's got your fly

I went down to the river on a Saturday morn
A-lookin' around just to see who's born
I found a little chicken down on his knees
I went up and yelled to him, "Please, please, please!"
He said, "Don't ya tell Henry
Don't ya tell Henry
Don't ya tell Henry
Apple's got your fly"

I went down to the corner at a-half past ten
I's lookin' around, I wouldn't say when
I looked down low, I looked above
And who did I see but the one I love
She said, "Don't ya tell Henry
Don't ya tell Henry
Don't ya tell Henry
Apple's got your fly"

Now, I went down to the beanery at half past twelve

不要告诉亨利

不要告诉亨利
苹果上落了你的苍蝇

星期六清早,我去河边
环顾下四周,看看有没有人出现
就看见一个胆小鬼在那儿跪着
我走过去冲他喊:"起来,起来,起来!"
他说:"不要告诉亨利
不要告诉亨利
不要告诉亨利
说苹果上落了你的苍蝇"

十点半,我去街拐角
我四处张望,不会说是何时
我往下看看,我往上看
而我看见的人,只有我爱的那位
她说:"不要告诉亨利
不要告诉亨利
不要告诉亨利
说苹果上落了你的苍蝇"

然后,十二点半,我去了小餐馆

A-lookin' around just to see myself
I spotted a horse and a donkey, too
I looked for a cow and I saw me a few
They said, "Don't ya tell Henry
Don't ya tell Henry
Don't ya tell Henry
Apple's got your fly"

Now, I went down to the pumphouse the other night
A-lookin' around, it was outa sight
I looked high and low for that big ol' tree
I did go upstairs but I didn't see nobody but me
I said, "Don't ya tell Henry
Don't ya tell Henry
Don't ya tell Henry
Apple's got your fly"

环顾四周,只看见我自己
也认出一匹马和一头驴
我想找头牛,还真看到了几头
它们说:"不要告诉亨利
不要告诉亨利
不要告诉亨利
说苹果上落了你的苍蝇"

然后,前两天的夜里,我去了泵房
环顾四周,可它却不见了
我上下望着,找那棵高大的老树
我确实上了楼,但除了我,我没看见人
我说:"不要告诉亨利
不要告诉亨利
不要告诉亨利
说苹果上落了你的苍蝇"

NOTHING WAS DELIVERED

Nothing was delivered
And I tell this truth to you
Not out of spite or anger
But simply because it's true
Now, I hope you won't object to this
Giving back all of what you owe
The fewer words you have to waste on this
The sooner you can go

Nothing is better, nothing is best
Take heed of this and get plenty of rest

Nothing was delivered
But I can't say I sympathize
With what your fate is going to be
Yes, for telling all those lies
Now you must provide some answers
For what you sell has not been received

还什么都未交付 [1]

还什么都未交付
我告诉你这事实
不是出于怨和怒
就只因为这是真的
现在,我希望你不会反对
把你欠的都还回来
你越少废话
就越早可以离开

没有什么更好,没有什么最好
你给我听好了,一边好好歇着

还什么都未交付
可我不能说我会同情
你即将到来的命运
是的,为了你撒的那些谎
现在你必须为你卖了却没到的货
提供解决办法

---

[1] 美国当代著名乐评人格雷尔·马库斯提到:"它缓慢从容的节拍、迪伦冷静的牛仔声线、响亮的钢琴声,同样是任何人所听过的、对胖子多米诺(Fats Domino)的《蓝莓山》("Blueberry Hill")的最佳改写。"

And the sooner you come up with them
The sooner you can leave

Nothing is better, nothing is best
Take heed of this and get plenty rest

(Now you know)
Nothing was delivered
And it's up to you to say
Just what you had in mind
When you made ev'rybody pay
No, nothing was delivered
Yes, 'n' someone must explain
That as long as it takes to do this
Then that's how long that you'll remain

Nothing is better, nothing is best
Take heed of this and get plenty rest

你越早提出来
就越早可以离开

没有什么更好,没有什么最好
你给我听好了,一边好好歇着

(现在你知道了吧)
还什么都未交付
随你爱说不说
当你让每个人交钱时
你心里在想什么
没有,还什么都没交付
是的,必须有人解释
就只需要这样
然后你就可以滚蛋

没有什么更好,没有什么最好
你给我听好了,一边好好歇着

OPEN THE DOOR, HOMER

Now, there's a certain thing
That I learned from Jim
That he'd always make sure I'd understand
And that is that there's a certain way
That a man must swim
If he expects to live off
Of the fat of the land
Open the door, Homer
I've heard it said before
Open the door, Homer
I've heard it said before
But I ain't gonna hear it said no more

Now, there's a certain thing
That I learned from my friend, Mouse
A fella who always blushes

开门,荷马 [1]

哎,有这么件事
我是从吉姆那儿知道的
他一直在确认我是否听懂了
他说一个人必须游
以某种方式游
如果他指望过上
地肥物美的生活
开门,荷马
这事情我听过
开门,荷马
这事情我听过
可我不会再听到了

现在,有这么件事
我从朋友"老鼠"那儿知道的
他是一个总爱红脸的伙计

---

[1] 这首歌的副歌部分源自黑人歌舞杂耍中的歌曲《开门,理查德》("Open the Door, Richard")。迪伦演唱时也将"开门,荷马"唱作"开门,理查德"。迪伦传记作者克林顿·海林认为,"荷马"这个名字是迪伦的朋友理查德·法里纳(Richard Fariña)的绰号。法里纳在1966年4月死于摩托车事故,同年7月迪伦也在摩托车事故中受伤。

And that is that ev'ryone
Must always flush out his house
If he don't expect to be
Goin' 'round housing flushes
Open the door, Homer
I've heard it said before
Open the door, Homer
I've heard it said
But I ain't gonna hear it said no more

"Take care of all your memories"
Said my friend, Mick
"For you cannot relive them
And remember when you're out there
Tryin' to heal the sick
That you must always
First forgive them"
Open the door, Homer
I've heard it said before
Open the door, Homer
I've heard it said before
But I ain't gonna hear it said no more

他说每个人
都应该把自己的房子冲干净
如果他不想
到处去清洗房子
开门,荷马
这事情我听过
开门,荷马
这事情我听过
可我不会再听到了

"照看好你所有的记忆"
朋友米克说
"因为你不可能重新经历
记住,当你到了那儿
试图救治病人时
你必须永远
先原谅他们"
开门,荷马
这事情我听过
开门,荷马
这事情我听过
可我不会再听到了

LONG-DISTANCE OPERATOR

Long-distance operator
Place this call, it's not for fun
Long-distance operator
Please, place this call, you know it's not for fun
I gotta get a message to my baby
You know, she's not just anyone

There are thousands in the phone booth
Thousands at the gate
There are thousands in the phone booth
Thousands at the gate
Ev'rybody wants to make a long-distance call
But you know they're just gonna have to wait

If a call comes from Louisiana
Please, let it ride
If a call comes from Louisiana
Please, let it ride
This phone booth's on fire

长途接线员 [1]

长途接线员
接通这电话吧,这可不是闹着玩儿
长途接线员
求你接通这电话,你知道这不是闹着玩儿
我有个消息要给我宝贝儿
你知道,她可不是一般人

电话亭有数千人
数千人在门口
电话亭有数千人
数千人在门口
每个人都想打长途
但是你知道他们只能再等等

如果从路易斯安那来了电话
求你,让它通过
如果从路易斯安那来了电话
求你,让它通过
这电话亭要着火了

---

[1] 迈克尔·格雷指出,歌名取自美国蓝调歌手小米尔顿(Little Milton)1959 年的同名歌曲。

It's getting hot inside

Ev'rybody wants to be my friend
But nobody wants to get higher
Ev'rybody wants to be my friend
But nobody wants to get higher
Long-distance operator
I believe I'm stranglin' on this telephone wire

里面越来越热

人人都想做我朋友
但是没人想飞得更高
人人都想做我朋友
但是没人想飞得更高
长途接线员
我相信我就要勒死在这电话线上

THIS WHEEL'S ON FIRE
(WITH RICK DANKO)

If your mem'ry serves you well
We were goin' to meet again and wait
So I'm goin' to unpack all my things
And sit before it gets too late
No man alive will come to you
With another tale to tell
But you know that we shall meet again
If your mem'ry serves you well
This wheel's on fire
Rolling down the road
Best notify my next of kin
This wheel shall explode!

这车轮烧起来了

（与里克·丹科合作）[1]

如果你的记性足够

那么我们应该会再见，现在需要等待

所以我要打开我所有的东西

坐下来，以免为时已晚

这世上没有活人会来找你

给你讲述另一个传说

但是你知道我们将会再见

如果你的记性足够

这车轮烧起来了

沿着道路滚动

最好去通知我的亲人

这车轮就要爆炸！

---

[1] 里克·丹科(Rick Danko)回忆："他(迪伦)给了我用打字机打出的《这车轮烧起来了》的歌词。那时我正在自学弹钢琴……某些我前一天在钢琴上创作的音乐，似乎正好跟迪伦的歌词相配。我加工了措辞和旋律。然后迪伦和我一起写了副歌部分。"歌名令人联想到迪伦1966年发生的摩托车事故。安迪·吉尔和罗伯特·谢尔顿都指出，这首歌呼应了《李尔王》第四幕中李尔王对小女儿考狄利娅说的话："你是一个有福的灵魂；我却缚在一个烈火的车轮上，我自己的眼泪也像熔铅一样灼痛我的脸。"（朱生豪译文）谢尔顿还指出，"车轮"意象与黑人灵歌《以西结看到了轮子》("Ezekiel Saw The Wheel")相关联。

If your mem'ry serves you well
I was goin' to confiscate your lace
And wrap it up in a sailor's knot
And hide it in your case
If I knew for sure that it was yours . . .
But it was oh so hard to tell
But you knew that we would meet again
If your mem'ry serves you well
This wheel's on fire
Rolling down the road
Best notify my next of kin
This wheel shall explode!

If your mem'ry serves you well
You'll remember you're the one
That called on me to call on them
To get you your favors done
And after ev'ry plan had failed
And there was nothing more to tell
You knew that we would meet again
If your mem'ry served you well
This wheel's on fire
Rolling down the road
Best notify my next of kin
This wheel shall explode!

如果你的记性足够
那么我应该没收掉你的蕾丝
用水手结包起来
藏在你的箱子里
假若我确定那是你的……
但是啊这很难说
但是你曾知道我们应该会再见
如果你的记性足够
这车轮烧起来了
沿着道路滚动
最好去通知我的亲人
这车轮就要爆炸！

如果你的记性足够
那么你会记得，正是你
召唤我，去召唤他们
前来领受你的恩泽
在每个计划都已经失败
而再没有更多的话可说
你曾知道我们应该会再见
如果你的记性足够
这车轮烧起来了
沿着道路滚动
最好去通知我的亲人
这车轮就要爆炸！

SIGN ON THE CROSS

Now, I try, oh for so awf'ly long
And I just try to be
And now, oh it's a gold mine
But it's so fine
Yes, but I know in my head
That we're all so misled
And it's that ol' sign on the cross
That worries me

Now, when I was just a bawlin' child
I saw what I wanted to be
And it's all for the sake
Of that picture I should see
But I was lost on the moon
As I heard that front door slam
And that old sign on the cross
Still worries me

Well, it's that old sign on the cross
Well, it's that old key to the kingdom
Well, it's that old sign on the cross
Like you used to be

十字架上的名号

哦,我努力,啊这么久了
我只是努力地活着
那么现在,噢这是座金矿
这样可真不错
是啊,但是我心里清楚
我们都被误导了
是十字架上的那个古老名号
令我烦忧

话说,当我还是个爱哭的孩子时
就知道了我要成为哪种人
而这一切都是因为
我应该看到了那个图像
但是我迷失在月球上
此时我听见前门砰地关上
而十字架上的那个古老名号
依然令我烦忧

哦,是十字架上的那个古老名号
哦,是开启王国的那把古老钥匙
哦,是十字架上的那个古老名号
就像你从前那样

But, when I hold my head so high
As I see my ol' friends go by
And it's still that sign on the cross
That worries me

Well, it seem to be the sign on the cross. Ev'ry day, ev'ry night,
see the sign on the cross just layin' up on top of the hill. Yes,
we thought it might have disappeared long ago, but I'm here
to tell you, friends, that I'm afraid it's lyin' there still. Yes, just a
little time is all you need, you might say, but I don't know 'bout
that any more, because the bird is here and you might want
to enter it, but, of course, the door might be closed. But I just
would like to tell you one time, if I don't see you again, that the
thing is, that the sign on the cross is the thing you might need
the most.

Yes, the sign on the cross
Is just a sign on the cross
Well, there is some on every chisel
And there is some in the championship, too
Oh, when your, when your days are numbered
And your nights are long
You might think you're weak
But I mean to say you're strong
Yes you are, if that sign on the cross
If it begins to worry you

但是，当我把头抬这么高
看到我的老友一个个走过
依然是十字架上的那个名号
令我烦忧

是的，那看起来就是十字架上的那个名号。每一天，每一夜，看见十字架上的名号，就矗立在山顶。是的，我们以为它可能早就消失了，但是现在我告诉你，朋友，恐怕它还在那儿立着呢。是的，你可能会说，你只是需要一些时间，但我不再那么确定，因为那只鸟在这儿，而你或许想进入其中，不过，当然，门也许关着。然而，我只想告诉你一次，假如我再也见不到你，我要说的是：十字架上的那个名号，可能是你最需要的东西。

是的，十字架上的名号
只不过是十字架上的一个名号
哦，每一把凿子上都有
而且那锦标里也有
啊，当你的，当你的日子屈指可数
而黑夜漫长
你也许会以为你很虚弱
但我想说你很刚强
是的你很刚强，假如十字架上的那个名号
假如它开始令你烦忧

Well, that's all right because sing a song
And all your troubles will pass right on through

好吧,这都没什么,因为唱首歌
你的所有烦恼就都将过去

QUINN THE ESKIMO
(THE MIGHTY QUINN)

Ev'rybody's building the big ships and the boats
Some are building monuments
Others, jotting down notes
Ev'rybody's in despair
Ev'ry girl and boy
But when Quinn the Eskimo gets here
Ev'rybody's gonna jump for joy
Come all without, come all within
You'll not see nothing like the mighty Quinn

I like to do just like the rest, I like my sugar sweet
But guarding fumes and making haste
It ain't my cup of meat
Ev'rybody's 'neath the trees
Feeding pigeons on a limb

爱斯基摩人魁恩 [1]
（威猛魁恩）

每个人都在造大船小艇

也有的在建纪念碑

其他的，匆匆记下笔记

每个人都很绝望

每个女孩和男孩

但是等爱斯基摩人魁恩一到

每个人都会高兴得蹦起来

外面的都来吧，里面的都来吧

你不会再见到像威猛魁恩这样的人物

我喜欢像其他人一样做，我喜欢我的糖很甜

但是守着烟气或者仓皇奔走

都不是我的菜 [2]

每一个人都在树荫下

喂那树枝上的鸽子

---

[1] "爱斯基摩人"为"因纽特人"的旧称，现渐趋弃用，为与原作对应，未做修改。迪伦曾在卡梅伦·克罗对他的访谈中提到这首歌，说"我想这是某种童谣吧"。一般认为歌词中的主角源自美国演员安东尼·奎恩在1960年上映的电影《雪海冰上人》中扮演的因纽特人一角。

[2] 本句化用"my cup of tea"，意思是不合我胃口，非我所爱。

But when Quinn the Eskimo gets here
All the pigeons gonna run to him
Come all without, come all within
You'll not see nothing like the mighty Quinn

A cat's meow and a cow's moo, I can recite 'em all
Just tell me where it hurts yuh, honey
And I'll tell you who to call
Nobody can get no sleep
There's someone on ev'ryone's toes
But when Quinn the Eskimo gets here
Ev'rybody's gonna wanna doze
Come all without, come all within
You'll not see nothing like the mighty Quinn

但是等爱斯基摩人魁恩一到
所有的鸽子都将奔向他
外面的都来吧,里面的都来吧
你不会再见到像威猛魁恩这样的人物

猫的喵喵和牛的哞哞,我都能背诵
只要告诉我你哪儿疼,亲爱的
我就会告诉你该喊谁来
所有的人都睡不着
每个人的脚趾都被人踩着
但是等爱斯基摩人魁恩一到
每个人都要打起瞌睡
外面的都来吧,里面的都来吧
你不会再见到像威猛魁恩这样的人物

I SHALL BE RELEASED

They say ev'rything can be replaced
Yet ev'ry distance is not near
So I remember ev'ry face
Of ev'ry man who put me here
I see my light come shining
From the west unto the east
Any day now, any day now
I shall be released

They say ev'ry man needs protection
They say ev'ry man must fall
Yet I swear I see my reflection
Some place so high above this wall
I see my light come shining
From the west unto the east
Any day now, any day now
I shall be released

Standing next to me in this lonely crowd

我将获得自由

他们说万物皆可取代
然而每段距离都不近
因此我记住了,把我丢到这里来的
每个人的每张脸
我看见我的灯亮起来
从西直到东
不一定哪天,不一定哪天
我将获得自由

他们说人人需要保护
他们说人人都有跌倒的时候
然而我发誓我看见了自己的倒影
在远高于这墙的某处
我看见我的灯亮起来
从西直到东
不定哪天,不定哪天
我将获得自由

这一片孤独人群,站我旁边的 [1]

---

[1] "这一片孤独人群,站我旁边的",指涉美国社会学家大卫·理斯曼(David Riesman)的著作《孤独的人群》(*The Lonely Crowd*)。

Is a man who swears he's not to blame
All day long I hear him shout so loud
Crying out that he was framed
I see my light come shining
From the west unto the east
Any day now, any day now
I shall be released

是一个发誓他不该受责罚的人
终日我听他大声叫喊
哭诉自己是被陷害的
我看见我的灯亮起来
从西直到东
不定哪天,不定哪天
我将获得自由

GET YOUR ROCKS OFF!

You know, there's two ol' maids layin' in the bed
One picked herself up an' the other one, she said:
"Get your rocks off!
Get your rocks off! (Get 'em off!)
Get your rocks off! (Get 'em off!)
Get your rocks off-a me! (Get 'em off!)"

Well, you know, there late one night up on Blueberry Hill
One man turned to the other man and said, with a blood-curdlin' chill, he said:
"Get your rocks off! (Get 'em off!)
Get your rocks off! (Get 'em off!)
Get your rocks off! (Get 'em off!)
Get your rocks off-a me! (Get 'em off!)"

Well, you know, we was layin' down around Mink Muscle Creek
One man said to the other man, he began to speak, he said:
"Get your rocks off! (Get 'em off!)
Get your rocks off! (Get 'em off!)
Get your rocks off! (Get 'em off!)

把你的石头拿开![1]

你知道,有两个老女仆躺在床上
一个爬起来而另一个,她说:
"把你的石头拿开!
把你的石头拿开!(拿开!)
把你的石头拿开!(拿开!)
把你的石头从我身上拿开!(拿开!)"

哦,你知道,有一天深夜在蓝莓山
一个人转向另一个人说,以冻结血液的寒冷,
　他说:
"把你的石头拿开!(拿开!)
把你的石头拿开!(拿开!)
把你的石头拿开!(拿开!)
把你的石头从我身上拿开!(拿开!)"

哦,你知道,我们当时躺在貂肉溪附近
一个人对另一个人说,他开口了,他说:
"把你的石头拿开!(拿开!)
把你的石头拿开!(拿开!)
把你的石头拿开!(拿开!)

---

[1] "把你的石头拿开",俚语中指高潮,又指享受某事物。

Get your rocks off-a me! (Get 'em off!)"

Well, you know, we was cruisin' down the highway in a Greyhound bus
All kinds-a children in the side road, they was hollerin' at us, sayin':
"Get your rocks off! (Get 'em off!)
Get your rocks off! (Get 'em off!)
Get your rocks off! (Get 'em off!)
Get your rocks off-a me!"

把你的石头从我身上拿开!（拿开!）"

哦,你知道,我们当时坐着灰狗巴士在公路
　巡游
各种孩子在小路上,冲着我们叫嚷,说:
"把你们的石头拿开!（拿开!）
把你们的石头拿开!（拿开!）
把你们的石头拿开!（拿开!）
把你们的石头从我身上拿开!"

SILENT WEEKEND

Silent weekend
My baby she gave it to me
Silent weekend
My baby she gave it to me
She's actin' tough and hardy
She says it ain't my party
And she's leavin' me in misery

Silent weekend
My baby she took me by surprise
Silent weekend
My baby she took me by surprise
She's rockin' and a-reelin'
Head up to ceiling
An' swinging with some other guys

Silent weekend
Oh Lord, I wish Monday would come
Silent weekend
Oh Lord, I sure wish Monday would come
She's uppity, she's rollin'
She's in the groove, she's strolling

不说话的周末

不说话的周末
我的宝贝给了我
不说话的周末
我的宝贝给了我
她态度强硬
说"这不是我的派对"
她丢下了我留在痛苦中

不说话的周末
我的宝贝让我吃一惊
不说话的周末
我的宝贝让我吃一惊
她摇摆又旋转
头冲上了天花板
和别的男人一起晃着

不说话的周末
主啊,我希望星期一到来
不说话的周末
主啊,我真希望星期一到来
她傲慢,她转圈
她乐颠颠,她溜达漫步

Over to the jukebox playin' deaf and dumb

Well, I done a whole lotta thinkin' 'bout a whole lot of cheatin'
And I, maybe I did some just to please
But I just walloped a lotta pizza after makin' our peace
Puts ya down on bended knees

Silent weekend
Man alive, I'm burnin' up on my brain
Silent weekend
Man alive, I'm burnin' up on my brain
She knows when I'm just teasin'
But it's not likely in the season
To open up a passenger train

到自动点唱机边,装聋作哑

嗯,对这许许多多欺骗我想了许多许多
而我,也许我犯下的事只是为了取悦
但是在我们和好后我捶打了许多比萨
这让你双膝跪地

不说话的周末
我还活着,脑子快烧完了
不说话的周末
我还活着,脑子快烧完了
她知道我什么时候是闹着玩
而这大概不会是
打开旅客列车门的时节

SANTA FE

Santa Fe, dear, dear, dear, dear, dear Santa Fe
My woman needs it ev'ryday
She promised this a-lad she'd stay
She's rollin' up a lotta bread to toss away

She's in Santa Fe, dear, dear, dear, dear, dear Santa Fe
Now she's opened up an old maid's home
She's proud, but she needs to roam
She's gonna write herself a roadside poem about Santa Fe

Santa Fe, dear, dear, dear, dear, dear Santa Fe
Since I'm never gonna cease to roam
I'm never, ever far from home
But I'll build a geodesic dome and sail away

Don't feel bad, no, no, no, no, don't feel bad
It's the best food I've ever had
Makes me feel so glad
That she's cooking in a homemade pad
She never caught a cold so bad when I'm away

圣菲[1]

圣菲,亲爱、亲爱、亲爱、亲爱、亲爱的圣菲
我的女人每天都需要它
她答应这小伙儿她会留下
她卷了很多面包扔掉

她在圣菲,亲爱、亲爱、亲爱、亲爱、亲爱的圣菲
这会儿她开张了老姑娘之家
她很骄傲,但是她需要漂泊
她要给自己写一首关于圣菲的路边诗

圣菲,亲爱、亲爱、亲爱、亲爱、亲爱的圣菲
既然我永远不会停止漂泊
那么我从来、从来不曾远离家
但我会造一座网格球顶,然后远航

不要难过,不、不、不、不、不要难过
这是我吃过的最好的美食
我特别高兴的是
她用自制隔热垫做饭
我不在的时候她从未得过这么重的感冒

---

[1] 圣菲,美国新墨西哥州的首府。

Santa Fe, dear, dear, dear, dear, dear, dear Santa Fe

My shrimp boat's in the bay

I won't have my nature this way

And I'm leanin' on the wheel each day to drift away from

Santa Fe, dear, dear, dear, dear, dear Santa Fe

My sister looks good at home

She's lickin' on an ice cream cone

She's packin' her big white comb

What does it weigh?

圣菲，亲爱、亲爱、亲爱、亲爱、亲爱的圣菲
我的捕虾船在海湾
我不想我的本性变成这样
每一天我都倚靠在轮舵上，让船漂远

圣菲，亲爱、亲爱、亲爱、亲爱、亲爱的圣菲
我妹妹在家看来不错
她在舔冰激凌蛋筒
正在收起她的大白梳子
它有多重？